COGNITIVE BEHAVIORAL THERAPY AND MINDFULNESS

2 BOOKS IN 1

OLIVIA TELFORD

COGNITIVE BEHAVIORAL THERAPY
AND MINDFULNESS: 2 Books in 1
by Olivia Telford

© Copyright 2021 by Olivia Telford

All Rights Reserved.

ISBN: 979-8594264090

ALSO BY OLIVIA TELFORD

*Hygge: Discovering The Danish Art Of Happiness –
How To Live Cozily And Enjoy Life's Simple Pleasures*

*The Art of Minimalism: A Simple Guide to Declutter
and Organize Your Life*

Hygge and The Art of Minimalism: 2 Books in 1

COGNITIVE BEHAVIORAL THERAPY

Simple Techniques **to Instantly Overcome Depression, Relieve Anxiety, and Rewire Your Brain**

Olivia Telford

CONTENTS

INTRODUCTION

D o you have a friend or relative who is always happy, self-accepting, and optimistic? Perhaps you've asked yourself what their secret is! Why can some people ride the stormy seas of life and stay smiling, while others spiral down into despair whenever something goes wrong?

The answer is actually quite simple. It all comes down to the way they think. Upbeat, self-assured people know that how you see the world and yourself makes all the difference. They know that to lead a great life, you need to learn how to get your mind working for you, not against you.

In this book, you're going to discover how to transform your thinking and completely overhaul your relationships and mental health. It won't be easy, but you'll feel the difference within hours. Practice the exercises in these chapters, and every area of your life will change for the better.

This isn't a book about always looking on the bright side of life. Life is a mix of the good, the bad, and the ugly. Everyone struggles. There's no special technique that can take away the normal trials and tribulations of being alive. But you can learn to rewire your brain and take a new approach when you hit a bump in the road.

The approach we're going to focus on in this book is called Cognitive Behavior Therapy, more commonly known as CBT. CBT has been around for decades. It's a straightforward model that explains why we get stressed, depressed and anxious, and what to do about it. Even better, CBT is backed up by lots of research. We know it works.

Psychologists have shown that CBT is a powerful treatment for:[1]

- Depression
- Anxiety
- Obsessive-Compulsive Disorder (OCD) and intrusive thoughts
- Phobias
- Stress
- Addiction
- Procrastination

CBT improves your confidence, boosts your happiness, and can make you more satisfied with life in general.[2] If you've been feeling stuck lately and aren't sure how to move forward, CBT will give you clarity. You'll understand yourself better, move on from your past, and look toward a brighter future.

Let's get started!

JOIN OUR SUPPORT GROUP

To maximize the value you receive from this book, I highly encourage you to join our tight-knit community on Facebook. Here you will be able to connect and share strategies with others to continue your growth.

Taking this journey alone is not recommended, and this can be an excellent support network for you.

It would be great to connect with you there,

Olivia Telford

To Join, Visit:
www.pristinepublish.com/mindfulgroup

DOWNLOAD THE AUDIO VERSION OF THIS BOOK FREE

If you love listening to audiobooks on-the-go or would enjoy a narration as you read along, I have great news for you. You can download the audiobook version of *Cognitive Behavioral Therapy and Mindfulness* for FREE (Regularly $19.95) just by signing up for a FREE 30-day Audible trial!

Visit: www.pristinepublish.com/audiobooks

YOUR FREE GIFT - 10 MINUTE MEDITATION

'm sorry to be the bearer of bad news, but life isn't about you! And the moment you accept this is when you will truly start living. We live in a world that justifies selfishness, and everything is about the self. The dominant thought process goes, "What am I going to get out of this? How is this situation going to benefit me? Who can I manipulate to give me what I want?" Society has trained us to believe that the more money we have, the more we can buy, and the happier we will be. But the evidence suggests that these things don't bring us fulfilment. Why? Because the ego is always going to want more. Some of the most successful people in the world are never satisfied. The private jet is never enough, multiple partners are never enough, a wardrobe full of designer clothes is never enough. The 25-room mansion, and properties all over the world are never enough. If the world has got it wrong, then what brings true contentment in life?

Knowing that your purpose on earth is to be a giver. We were created to be givers, to empty ourselves using our gifts and talents in order to make the world a better place. Our peace comes from living selflessly, and not selfishly. I believe that the root cause of the human condition is that we are not living the way we were created to live. We've been corrupted and it's causing us to malfunction. The physical manifestation of this is seen through anxiety, depression, stress, and the plethora of mental health issues that we suffer from. Have you noticed that the happiest people are those who have found their purpose, and that purpose is always connected to giving of themselves? That's because they are doing what they were created to do.

"This all sounds great," I hear you saying, "but what do I need to do to get to this point? How can I live a selfless life when I'm struggling with anxiety, overthinking, stress, and depression? I can barely make it through the day, let alone think about living for other people." May I submit to you that meditation is the key to freeing yourself from the mental prison you are currently locked in? Here's how.

Meditation helps you connect with your higher self. Right now, you are living far below your capabilities, but you are more powerful than you could ever imagine. Science proves that meditation rewires the brain. It strengthens certain areas in the brain and transforms your internal emotional state. It makes you more compassionate and improves your ability to focus. Why is that important? Because a wandering mind can't focus on the needs of others. Additionally, several studies have found that meditation is linked to compassionate behavior towards oneself and others. It basically makes us more altruistic, which is exactly what we need if we are going to live to our full potential.

Meditation will teach you how to disconnect from the world so you can connect with your inner world. How much time do you spend on social media connecting meaningfully with people you know? We know more about the lives of the latest celebrities than we do about ourselves. Some people have become so co-dependent that spending time alone scares them. Being continuously engaged has become the norm, and those who enjoy solitude are often ridiculed. But the irony is that solitude is the only way you can truly get to know yourself. Switching off the TV and putting down the phone to tune in to yourself is a terrifying prospect for some of us.

You're not alone. When I first started meditating, I was afraid of getting to know myself too. I was petrified of listening to the voices in my head because I'd spent most of my life running from them. The more I ran, the more I suffered, because I was running into the same like-minded people who didn't like themselves very much either. True love starts from within. If you don't love yourself, it's impossible to love anyone else. And how can you love yourself if you don't know yourself? It took me a while to get to know and love myself, and I'm still learning who I am. When I embraced solitude, and finally surrendered, I really started enjoying my own company. You've just got to take that leap of faith and do it because it works. I now have the peace and freedom I've always wanted. Meditation was a complete game changer for me; it even gave me the confidence to quit my job and start writing full time!

Unfortunately, meditation intimidates many people, and they have no idea how transformative it is. If you were to ask the average person what comes to mind when they think about meditation, they'll say something like, "A monk sitting on top of a hill thinking about nothing for hours." As you will discover, meditation is much more than the stereotypes portray. Furthermore, you can experience the full benefits by meditating for as little as ten minutes each day.

Do you want to enrich your life, free yourself from the burdens of anxiety, stress, and overthinking? Do you want to transcend the human mind and connect with the infinite source? Do you want to live an abundant life overflowing with peace, joy, and happiness? Do you want to find fulfilment in everything you do? Do you want to develop deeper relationships with your loved ones and improve your health? The information in this guide will help you achieve it. In this bonus e-book, you can expect to learn about the following:

- Exactly what meditation is and what it isn't
- The basics of meditation and the different types
- The health benefits of meditation
- Meditation techniques to help you overcome anxiety, stress, overthinking and insomnia

The aim of *10 Minute Meditation* is to take the fear out of meditation and make it accessible to all who desire to improve their lives on a deeper level. I truly believe that what you are about to read will radically transform your life.

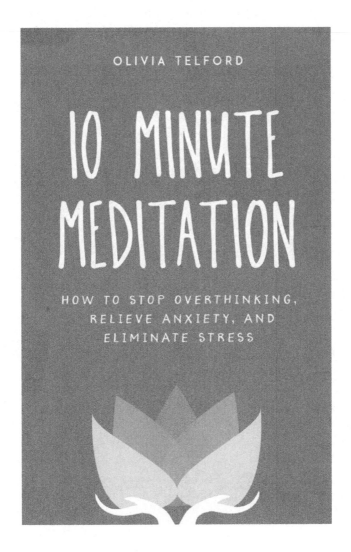

Get *10 Minute Meditation* for Free by Visiting

www.pristinepublish.com/meditationbonus

CHAPTER 1:

WHAT IS CBT?

Psychologists know that our genetic makeup, environment, and upbringing all shape our personalities.[3] Some of us are naturally more or less optimistic than others. However, the stories we tell ourselves about the world, ourselves, and life in general also make a big difference.

In this chapter, you'll discover exactly how this works.

WHY YOUR BRAIN IS BOTH YOUR BEST FRIEND & YOUR WORST ENEMY

Humans are blessed—and cursed—with the ability to tell stories. We aren't very good at observing situations as they really are, particularly when they involve someone or something we care about. Our brains are quick to impose some kind of meaning or narrative on any event, even if it leaves us feeling worse.

Your brain, which is supposed to be on your side, can actually make your life harder. Once you understand how this works, you can start applying the principles of CBT to take back control over your own thoughts.

TELLING STORIES – AN EXAMPLE

Imagine you are walking down the street. It's a beautiful sunny day, and you're feeling good. You see one of your friends ahead of you on the sidewalk, so you call out their name, but they don't turn around. They ignore you completely and keep on walking.

How would you respond?

You might think, "Oh, they didn't hear me. That's a shame."

Or perhaps you might think, "Oh dear, maybe something has upset them. They usually love to stop and chat."

Or maybe you'd think, "My so-called friend is avoiding me. Typical! Why is it so hard for me to maintain friendships?"

However you'd respond, keep in mind that the facts remain exactly the same. You called out to someone you knew, they didn't turn around, and they walked away. But the story you tell yourself about the event will change how you feel.

If you tell yourself that your friend probably didn't hear you, your mood won't change much. You will get on with your day and perhaps text them later to mention that you saw them in town.

If you jump to the conclusion that your friend must have been upset, you may feel concerned and get in touch to make sure they are OK.

If you decide that your friend ignored you because they no longer want to talk to you, you'll feel terrible. You might avoid your friend because, in your mind, they've made it clear that they don't like you anymore.

It's your interpretation of a situation that makes just as much of a difference as what actually happened.[4]

Exercise: What Was the Last Story You Told Yourself?

Think back over the last 24 hours. Have you been telling yourself any stories that left you feeling sad or anxious? Could you have interpreted those situations in a different way that would have left you feeling good, or at least OK?

CBT is all about changing the stories you tell yourself. Using the techniques in this book, you'll learn how.

The Key Assumptions of CBT[5]

Every type of therapy is based on a set of assumptions. You can think of these assumptions as a kind of model of the human mind.

CBT practitioners believe:

1. Depression, anxiety, stress, and bad habits are caused and sustained by core beliefs we hold about ourselves, thinking errors, or both.

   When we have irrational, negative beliefs about ourselves, other people, and the world in general, we start to tell ourselves stories that make us unhappy, anxious, and dissatisfied.

2. It's easy to fall into the trap of using the same thinking errors over and over again.

   For example, if you have depression, you probably see the world as a bleak, hopeless place that offers you nothing but sorrow. Your view of everything gets darker, you withdraw from situations that could make you feel better, and the cycle continues.

3. The way we see the world affects our behavior.

   If we view the world through a distorted lens, we won't adapt well to our environment or life's challenges. For instance, if you have anxiety, the stories you tell yourself about the world—that it is dangerous, for example—might make you reluctant to go outside.

4. It's possible to hone in on destructive thoughts and change them.

   With the right techniques, we can pin down how and why our thinking patterns make us feel so bad. We can then choose to change them.

5. Although someone's past might play a role in shaping their cognitive distortions, it's more productive to focus on the present.

   A CBT therapist might talk about a client's childhood to work out where their negative core beliefs come from, but they encourage clients not to dwell on them.[6] The exercises in this book don't require you to analyze your past in much depth. The emphasis is on helping yourself right now, so you can make progress quickly.

WHERE DID CBT COME FROM?

CBT started with the work of Albert Ellis and Aaron Beck in the 1950s and 1960s.[7] Since then, other psychologists and psychiatrists have put together their own techniques and treatment programs based on these ideas.

ELLIS' ABC MODEL

In 1955, an American psychologist called Albert Ellis proposed his ABC model.[8] He believed that external events don't automatically trigger negative emotional responses. What really matters is the belief someone has about that event. We saw an example earlier in this chapter when you imagined how you'd feel if a friend ignored you in the street.

In the ABC model, "A" stands for external or activating events, "B" stands for beliefs, and "C" stands for consequences, which refers to emotions and behaviors. Our beliefs act like filters, and they determine how we react to our circumstances.

What makes this model so special is that it can help you feel better even when you don't have much, or any, control over your environment. For instance, if you are in a job you hate, learning to think differently about your circumstances can help make you feel better as you work to find a new position.

Ellis developed his own brand of therapy, called Rational Emotive Behavior Therapy (REBT). REBT teaches clients how to identify their unhelpful beliefs, challenge them, and replace them with more constructive ways of seeing the world.[9]

BECK'S COGNITIVE THERAPY MODEL

In the 1960s, American psychiatrist Aaron T. Beck was researching depression. Beck started his career as a psychoanalyst. His training in psychoanalytic theory and therapy taught him that mental distress was caused by unconscious processes. But he wasn't convinced. He didn't think it was necessary to probe a patient's subconscious mind to find the source of their problems. He thought that open, honest discussion about their conscious thoughts was more helpful.

After talking to many patients, he concluded that people with depression tend to experience three types of negative thoughts:[10]

1. Negative thoughts and ideas about themselves.
2. Negative thoughts and ideas about the world.
3. Negative thoughts and ideas about the future.

He referred to these three types of thoughts as the "cognitive triad."

Beck noticed that his patients didn't feel able to control these thoughts. He labeled them "automatic thoughts" because they seemed to appear without warning. Some people refer to these as "ANTs," which stands for "Automatic Negative Thoughts."

In the early days, he called his treatment "cognitive therapy" because it focused on a patient's thoughts. However, later on, he and other professionals started looking at the relationship between thoughts and behavior, so "cognitive therapy" became "CBT."

Over a career spanning several decades, Beck carried out research with hundreds of patients. He and his colleagues discovered that CBT can be used to treat other disorders, including anxiety, eating disorders, schizophrenia, and bipolar disorder.

CBT TODAY

Ellis and Beck were CBT pioneers, and their efforts laid the foundations for other approaches that are considered offshoots of CBT.

Here are just three examples:

1. Dialectical Behavior Therapy (DBT)
   Developed in the 1980s by Dr. Marsha Linehan, DBT teaches clients how to accept their symptoms and problems while making positive change.[11] DBT is delivered as a structured course that usually lasts around a

year. Clients learn how to monitor their moods, identify the link between their thoughts and their feelings, and tolerate distress. They also learn how to think more rationally and apply everyday problem-solving skills.

DBT was originally developed for people with Borderline Personality Disorder (BPD), a condition marked by black-and-white thinking, mood swings, and rocky relationships. However, DBT techniques have also been used to treat other conditions.

People with BPD are prone to judging themselves and others harshly, with devastating consequences. DBT teaches them to step back from heated situations, weigh up all sides of an argument, and preserve relationships while still standing up for their wants and needs.

2. Acceptance and Commitment Therapy (ACT)[12]

As the name implies, ACT teaches clients how to come to terms with their problems and come up with solutions that fit their morals and values. Like traditional CBT, ACT entails facing your thoughts and feelings even if they make you uncomfortable.

The difference between ACT and other forms of CBT is that ACT emphasizes acceptance along with change. Unlike CBT practitioners, ACT therapists believe it isn't always a good idea to deliberately challenge negative thoughts. Instead, they teach clients how to spot their thoughts, tolerate them, and draw up healthy goals that align with their personal values.

3. Mindfulness Based Cognitive Therapy (MBCT)[13]

You've probably heard of mindfulness—it's become a huge buzzword in personal development circles. To be mindful is to deliberately slow down and notice what is happening around you. It's about focusing on the here and now, instead of ruminating about the past or worrying about the future.

MBCT is a structured 8-week program developed by Mark Williams, John Teasdale, and Zindel Segal. It's based on the work of mindfulness pioneer Jon Kabat-Zinn, whose research shows that meditation and other mindful activities can reduce stress and chronic pain. MBCT is especially effective for people who have suffered multiple episodes of depression. Mindfulness helps you spot unhelpful patterns of thinking and behavior before they take hold.

WHAT DO ALL THESE TREATMENTS HAVE IN COMMON?

Although these therapies use different techniques and are based on slightly different philosophies, they share a few key things in common. They all encourage clients to identify their negative thought processes, they all teach clients to become their own therapists, and they all encourage a pragmatic, goal-setting approach to behavior change.

In this book, you'll use a variety of techniques based on several different therapies that all fall under the CBT umbrella.

CBT IN THE THERAPY ROOM VS. SELF-HELP

Traditionally, talking therapy takes place between a client and a trained therapist. Most CBT interventions last around 8-12 weeks, although some people need more sessions. Therapy sessions usually last 50-60 minutes.

However, not everyone has the time or money for therapy. Even if you live in a country with free healthcare, you might have to wait a long time to see a clinician.

Self-help can be a great alternative. Research has shown that self-guided CBT can be an effective treatment for common mental health problems.[14] In the UK, the National Health Service (NHS) recommends self-guided CBT for some people diagnosed with mild to moderate mental health problems.

CBT ISN'T A MAGIC CURE

CBT requires effort. Whether you work through the techniques alone or with someone else, you have to put in the work before you see any results. Simply reading through the book won't change your life. You need to understand the concepts and be committed to practicing them over and over again. It takes time to change your thought patterns. Breaking habits is hard work.

HOMEWORK

Homework is a big part of CBT. CBT therapists often ask their clients to use worksheets and diaries, both during and between sessions. A therapist might ask a new client to keep a mood diary for a week or record their most frequent negative thoughts.

Every chapter of this book contains a few exercises to help you understand and benefit from CBT. Before you go any further, find a notebook and pen and keep them on hand. Whenever you start a new exercise or list, write the date at the top of the page.

You don't have to show your homework to anyone else. Your notebook is for your eyes only. If you live with other people, you might want to keep it locked or hidden away. If you really don't like writing, you could use a notetaking or voice recording app on your phone or computer instead.

Now that you know what CBT is about, it's time to start practicing some exercises that will make a big difference in your quality of life. In the next chapter, we'll see how CBT techniques can help you overcome symptoms of low mood and depression.

Summary

- The stories we tell ourselves about what is happening in our lives make a substantial difference in our mood.
- CBT is based on the idea that our thoughts (cognitions), feelings, and behaviors are all closely intertwined.
- By learning to challenge our unhelpful thoughts, we can feel better and choose new, healthier behaviors.
- CBT has inspired other therapies, including DBT and ACT.
- CBT can be given in a face-to-face setting, but self-help is also effective.
- Keeping notes and completing written exercises is a key part of CBT.

CHAPTER 2:

CBT FOR DEPRESSION

Depression is one of the world's leading causes of illness and disability. Around 15% of us will have at least one episode,[15] and suffering depression puts you at greater risk of experiencing it again.[16]

In this chapter, we'll look at how CBT practitioners view depression. You'll also learn how to lift your mood fast using proven CBT techniques.

What Is Depression?

Depression isn't the same as a feeling of sadness. It's a mental illness with a specific set of symptoms that can only be formally diagnosed by a trained medical professional.

To qualify for a diagnosis of depression, you need to experience at least five of the following symptoms for a minimum period of two weeks. One of these symptoms must be either a depressed mood or loss of pleasure.

Symptoms:[17]

1. A depressed mood that lasts throughout the day, most days of the week

2. Loss of interest and pleasure regarding everyday activities, including previously enjoyed hobbies
3. Significant (5%+) and unintentional weight change
4. Difficulty getting to sleep or sleeping too much
5. Feelings of restlessness or feeling slowed down
6. Loss of energy and fatigue
7. Feelings of excessive, inappropriate guilt and rumination over actual or perceived mistakes
8. Trouble thinking clearly, problems making decisions, or finding it hard to concentrate
9. Thoughts of death, suicide, or suicide ideation

Caution!

If you suspect you have depression, or are having thoughts of self-harm or suicide, you need to reach out to a doctor or therapist as soon as possible. Self-help guides can be very helpful, but they aren't a substitute for urgent medical care. You can always come back to this chapter when you have received a diagnosis and have started treatment as per your doctor's recommendations.

WHAT DO CBT THERAPISTS BELIEVE ABOUT DEPRESSION?

As you know, CBT is based on the idea that the way we see the world affects our mood and behavior. But how exactly can your thought patterns lead to depression?

In the last chapter, we saw how Beck's cognitive triad plays a key role in CBT theory. Beck devised two other concepts to explain what happens when someone is depressed.

Key Concept #1: Self Schemas

A schema is a set of beliefs and expectations about a person, thing, or scenario. We have schemas about everything.[18] For example, most of us have a restaurant schema. Your ideas about going out for a meal in a restaurant include expectations about menus, tables, chairs, servers, food, drinks, and so on.

Although every restaurant has its own décor, staff, and food, the basic principles are the same. If you've been to a few restaurants, you have a good idea of what to expect the next time. Schemas are useful because they help us plan ahead and respond to new environments. They help us understand how to behave appropriately around other people.

Just as you have a restaurant schema, you also have a "self-schema." As you may have guessed, a self-schema is a set of beliefs about who you are and how you should act.

Someone with a positive self-schema knows they aren't perfect, but they usually think of themselves as a basically good human being. On the other hand, people with depression often have negative self-schemas.

If you have a negative self-schema, you may have the following beliefs:

"I'm just not good enough."

"I'll never be successful, and I'll never get anywhere in life."

"Everyone leaves me, and I'll be lonely forever."

Beck thought that difficult childhood events could lead to a negative self-schema. For example, if a young boy is bullied at school for a long time, he may grow into a man who believes everyone hates him.

If you think poorly of yourself, you will be vulnerable to depression. A negative self-schema makes it hard to appreciate your achievements and enjoy relationships because you never quite believe you deserve them. Even when things are going well, you might find it hard to trust other people.

Exercise: Completing Sentences

Sentence completion exercises can help you uncover the negative self-schemas that are holding you back.

In your notebook, complete the following sentences. Don't overthink this. Write the first thing that comes to mind.

"I am the sort of person who..."

"In my experience, the world is..."

"When I think of the future, I think..."

This exercise can be quite illuminating. You might be shocked to discover just how negative your thoughts have become.

Your negative self-schemas might keep you trapped inside a cycle of negative thoughts and behaviors. For instance, if you always think that the future is bleak and that things will never get better, you might not bother to make plans or work toward goals.

Key Concept #2: Faulty Processing & Logical Errors

Negative self-schemas go hand-in-hand with logical errors. Logical errors are self-defeating patterns that keep you trapped in an unhealthy state of mind.

Here are a few of the most common logical errors, also known as "cognitive distortions:"[19,20]

1. Black and white thinking
   When we're depressed, we often lose sight of the fact that life is neither perfect nor terrible. Instead, we are

quick to judge things and people as "bad" or "good," including ourselves. Also known as polarized thinking, black and white thinking keeps you from appreciating the nuances of everyday life.

2. Overgeneralizing

If you tend to overgeneralize, you focus on one poor outcome or event and decide that it's bound to happen again. You assume that a single setback dooms you to a miserable future.

For example, let's say you give a presentation at work. It doesn't go very well. Your boss pulls you to one side and gives you advice on how to improve next time.

A non-depressed person might be a little down or disappointed for a while, but they would probably act on their boss' feedback and even thank them for it. However, someone with depression might assume that all their future presentations are doomed and that their whole professional future is in serious jeopardy because of their poor performance.

3. Fallacy of change

Most of us are guilty of trying to get other people to change. Unfortunately, expecting others to change just to suit your agenda will make everyone unhappy. If you are stuck in this cognitive distortion, you believe that everything in your life will be better if the rest of the world gives in to your demands.

For example, a man might believe that his marriage and life in general will improve if and when his wife joins a gym, works out more, and loses the weight she gained after they got married.

4. Just reward fallacy (or "Heaven's reward fallacy")

    As we all know, life isn't fair. However, that doesn't keep us from feeling resentful when things don't go our way. Many people with depression think that if they do everything right and treat others properly, they will somehow be rewarded.

    Unfortunately, if you hold this view, you'll be disappointed over and over again. Healthy people know that it's great to try your best, but we don't always have control over the final outcome. Other people may treat us well or poorly, and we cannot control their actions.

5. Emotional reasoning

    When you're in the grip of intense emotion, logical reasoning can fly out of the window. For example, if something makes you feel upset or scared, you might leap to the conclusion that it must be bad. For example, if a depressed person is nervous about going on a date, they might assume that this means it will go wrong and they probably shouldn't go at all.

6. "Shoulds"

    People with depression often use the word "should" a lot, both in reference to themselves and others.

    Even if you don't try to tell everyone else what to do, "shoulding" yourself isn't much better. Beating yourself up for not living up to a set of unrealistic or arbitrary standards will keep you locked in a state of self-criticism and depression.

7. Personalization

    When you personalize an outcome, you assume that you caused it, even if you have no evidence. For example, suppose that your partner didn't get the promotion they wanted. If your first thought is, "If I'd been nicer lately and less stressed, they would have gotten it, I'm a terrible person!" or something similar, that's personalization. When we're depressed, it feels as though we can't do anything right. Worse, it seems like everything is our fault.

8. Catastrophizing

   Also known as "blowing everything out of proportion" or "making mountains out of molehills," catastrophizing involves giving negative events or outcomes more weight than they deserve. When you catastrophize, you conjure up worst-case scenarios, usually in a matter of seconds.

   For example, suppose you forget to pick up your partner's suit from the dry cleaner on your way home from work, and only remember once you start cooking dinner. If you are a catastrophizer, you may tell yourself things like, "I'm such an awful partner! We'll get into a fight, they'll leave me, and then I'll be alone forever!"

9. Filtering

   When someone is overly optimistic about something, we say that they're wearing rose-colored glasses. If you're depressed, you're wearing gray-tinted glasses instead! If you focus on unpleasant details and ignore the bigger picture, you are filtering.

10. Blaming

    People with depression assume that others have the power to "make" them feel a particular way. But this is a fallacy.

    Suppose someone insults you. You might feel mildly offended, baffled, outraged, deeply upset, or something else entirely. What determines how you feel? Your approach to the situation. When you blame someone else for your own emotional state, you are surrendering your power.

11. Mind reading

Do you assume that you "just know" what someone else is thinking? Do you think you can tell when others are judging you? Mind reading can make you feel depressed, fast. For example, if you tell yourself, "Oh, so-and-so didn't return my email, she must think I'm completely incompetent and is avoiding me," there's a good chance you'll feel bad.

Depressed people are quick to assume that everyone is thinking the worst of them. In reality, most people go through their daily lives thinking only about themselves.

Exercise: What Logical Errors Do You Use?

As you read through the list above, did any errors stand out for you? Note that you can be very depressed and only use one or two of these distortions, so don't be surprised if you didn't recognize most items on the list. Over the next few days, challenge yourself to spot your distortions.

THE THREE STEPS TO MORE REALISTIC THINKING

You're about to learn a popular CBT technique that will let you take back control of your thoughts. It's called cognitive restructuring.

Cognitive restructuring isn't about living in denial or wishing your problems away. You don't have to force yourself to think happy thoughts all the time. The aim is to process your thoughts in a balanced, rational way that leaves you feeling better about yourself and life in general.

At first, cognitive restructuring might feel a little forced. It can be hard work, especially if you have been caught up in logical errors and self-loathing for a long time. The good news is that it gets easier the more you do it.

There are three steps:[21]

1. Identifying an unhelpful thought
2. Weighing up the evidence for and against the thought
3. Coming up with a rational, more helpful alternative

Let's look at each step in more detail.

Step #1: Identifying an Unhelpful Thought

Because negative thoughts are often automatic, it's hard to notice them. You can use your emotions as a signal that your thoughts are making you anxious. The next time you feel distressed or worried, ask yourself what you were thinking just before the emotion set in. Use your notebook as a thought record. Jot down the thought, together with a number denoting how strongly you believe it. A score of 0 means that you hardly believe it at all, and a score of 100 means you believe it completely.

Automatic negative thoughts (ANTs) are normally short, specific, and seem totally believable. However, if you look closely, you'll notice that they don't pop up after a sequence of logical thoughts. They tend to have a life of their own. You'll also realize that they usually involve logical errors, as listed earlier in this chapter.

Exercise: Spotting Your ANTs

If you are depressed, you likely have lots of ANTs. Tomorrow, keep a running tally throughout the day. Whenever a new ANT pops up, write it down. Every time it appears again, add another mark. Count up the marks. Are you very harsh on yourself?

Step #2: Weighing the Evidence

Your next task is to step back from your thought and work out whether it is actually true. No matter how believable an ANT may seem, it probably isn't grounded in fact. Ask yourself these questions:

- What would I say to someone else in this situation?
- If I didn't feel depressed, how would I look at the situation?
- How would someone who isn't depressed or anxious look at the situation?
- Is there any objective evidence that my thought is true?

In your notebook, draw up a table. Make four columns: "Thought," "Evidence for This Thought," "Evidence Against This Thought," and "More Helpful Way of Thinking About the Situation." Stick to facts, not subjective opinions.

Let's see how this exercise can work in practice. Suppose you were dating someone you really liked, but they suddenly ended the relationship, saying they didn't feel the two of you had good chemistry. You think to yourself, "I'll be alone forever, and no one likes me."

Here's what you might write in your table:

Thought: "I'll be alone forever, and no one likes me."

Evidence for This Thought:

- Someone ended a relationship I thought was going well, so this means they don't want to be with me.

Evidence Against This Thought:

- I have had friends and dates in the past. This means people enjoy my company.
- Most people have to date quite a lot before they find a long-term partner.
- Most people do not end up "alone forever."
- Not everyone would be a good match for me, and this is true for everyone else.

More Helpful Way of Thinking About the Situation:

- I am disappointed that the relationship didn't work out, but there are lots of other people to date.
- I can take some time to recover from this setback, then try meeting some new people.

Step #3: Coming Up with a Rational, More Helpful Alternative Thought

A good alternative thought is reasonable, fair, and compassionate.

In the example above, some good alternative thoughts might be:

I'm not in a relationship, but that doesn't mean I'll be alone forever.

I'm a bit lonely right now, but I know that some people like me.

Being rejected sucks, but I can keep trying until I find the right person for me.

Imagine that you are a judge in a court of law. Your job is to look at all the evidence and come to a sensible conclusion. If you find this exercise challenging, ask a trusted friend or relative to help you look at the situation from a different perspective.

Write down how you feel when you focus on your new thought. If it doesn't make you feel any better, repeat Step #2 above. There is always a more helpful way of thinking about your situation.

OTHER TOOLS TO HELP YOU FIGHT DEPRESSION

In this chapter, we've looked at how cognitive restructuring can help you feel better. In the next section, you'll learn about two other powerful CBT techniques to lift your mood.

SUMMARY

- Depression is a common mental illness. Symptoms include feelings of hopelessness and loss of interest in things you used to enjoy.
- CBT therapists believe that depression is caused by negative thoughts (the cognitive triad), negative self-schemas, and faulty thought processes.
- Automatic Negative Thoughts (ANTs) are a common problem in depression, but they can be conquered with the right CBT techniques.
- Cognitive restructuring exercises reframe your negative thoughts and replace them with a more constructive perspective.

CHAPTER 3:

BEHAVIORAL ACTIVATION & PROBLEM SOLVING

I n the last chapter, you learned how your self-schema, thoughts, and view of the world can keep you locked in a state of depression. You practiced two CBT techniques therapists often use with depressed patients: sentence completion tasks and cognitive restructuring.

In this chapter, you're going to pick up a couple more tools that will help you fight back against low moods and depression: Behavioral Activation (BA) and problem-solving.

BEHAVIORAL ACTIVATION (BA)

Depressed people often feel weighed down and apathetic. Even small, everyday tasks such as doing the laundry become daunting. Depression drains you of energy, leaving you asking, "What's the point in doing anything?"

As time goes on, you cut more activities from your daily life, which leaves you feeling even more depressed and worthless. Your motivation continues to dive. You start telling yourself things like, "I can't cope with anything," "I'll never get better," and "I don't enjoy anything anymore."

To break out of depression, you need to stop this cycle. The only way to regain control over your life is to deliberately engage in positive activity again, even when you don't want to. This strategy is known as behavioral activation, or BA.[22] The first step is to think of activities you used to enjoy, as outlined in the next exercise.

Exercise: Planning Positive Activities

Make a list of low-key activities you enjoyed before you developed depression. These activities could be as simple as watching a movie at home. Give yourself time to make your list because depression can make it harder to remember things.

Now plan when you can do three of these activities over the coming week. To begin with, 20 minutes is enough. Make a note of each session in your diary. It's just as important as any other commitment, so don't feel guilty about making time for yourself.

Don't expect to feel excited at this stage. Making this list probably felt like a chore. That's normal! The real progress comes when you follow through and keep a record, as explained in the next exercise.

Exercise: Pre- and Post-Activity Mood Record

Before you start a planned activity, make a note of your mood. Give yourself a score of 1-10, where a score of "1" means "very little energy or motivation" and "10" means "very excited and enthusiastic."

When you've finished, write down your score. Any increase, even if it's just one or two points, is a step in the right direction. Sometimes your score might not change at all. If you feel as though nothing is making you feel better, it may even go down. That's OK. It just means you need to change your planned activity, or perhaps try again another time.

Choose Activities that Move You Closer to the Person You Want to Be

BA is more effective if you choose activities that are in line with your goals and values. For instance, if you want to be more sociable, setting yourself the goal of chatting with an old friend for 10 minutes on the phone would be a great BA goal.[23]

Finally, make sure you are choosing activities you really want to do, not what you think you should be doing. For instance, don't set yourself the goal of cleaning the bathroom or doing the grocery shopping. Sure, these are important activities, but the point of BA is to help you re-engage with the things you enjoy.

You Don't Have to Look Forward to It, Just Do It Anyway

When you try BA, the little voice in your head might tell you unhelpful things like:

"This won't work. You never enjoy anything."
"It can't be this simple. It won't make you feel better."
"It might work for other people, but not for you."

The secret? Try it anyway. What's the worst that could happen? Even if you try an activity for 10 minutes and feel no different, you haven't lost out on anything. You can then try again the next day or try another activity. If you feel motivated on some days but not others, you can rest assured that this is completely normal.

Progress isn't always linear when it comes to recovering from depression. Some days, you'll feel hopeful. Others, you'll feel defeated before you even start. The trick is to just keep going.

When you complete your BA exercises, give yourself plenty of praise. You have every right to be proud!

Once you have some evidence that BA works for you, you can challenge these negative thoughts using the cognitive restructuring exercise outlined in the last chapter. Remember: you need to identify an unhelpful thought, look carefully at the evidence for and against it, and then come up with a healthier alternative thought.

WHEN TO GET SUPPORT

If you've tried BA exercises several times and they don't seem to be working for you, it may be a sign that you need further support from a therapist or doctor. Please don't think that you've failed. Sometimes, depression doesn't respond to self-help. If you feel very low or have no energy for even brief 10-minute activities, it's time to find a medical professional who can help you take the first steps to recovery.

DEPRESSION, PROBLEM-SOLVING & EMPOWERING YOURSELF

A little-known but very common problem in depression is having trouble making decisions. The good news is that you can sharpen your problem-solving skills. Problem-solving isn't always straightforward, and it can feel overwhelming when your mood is low. At the same time, devising solutions and putting them into practice is very empowering.[24]

When you realize that you don't need someone else to come along as rescue you, your self-esteem will grow. This will help you feel good about yourself, which in turn will help lift your mood.

Seven Steps to Problem Solving

1. Work out What the Problem is

   In some cases, it's obvious. For example, if you know that you need to choose a new school for your child, solving the problem is a matter of evaluating local schools and picking the best option. On the other hand, some problems aren't so easy to pin down. You might know that you are unhappy in a specific situation, but perhaps the details are a bit fuzzy.

   For instance, if you know that you dislike going into work, you'll need to think carefully about the underlying source of the issue. What is it about the environment or the work itself that is making you sad or depressed?

   Upon reflection, you may discover that the problem is, "I need to find a new job," or "I need to be more organized so that I can meet all my deadlines, and have a less stressful time at work."

   When you've narrowed down the problem, write it in your notebook. Well done! You're off to a good start.

2. Brainstorm a List of Potential Solutions

   Let your imagination run wild. Put aside half an hour to make a list of every solution you can think of. Don't worry if they seem strange or unlikely. You don't have to show this list to anyone.

   Get some outside input. Ask a couple of people you trust to help brainstorm with you. They will probably come up with some ideas you haven't thought of. When you are stuck in a depressed mood, your problem-solving abilities take a hit. It's easy to become locked into a single perspective.

If you have a serious problem, or you can't rely on anyone close to you to help out, get some advice from a specialist. Depending on your problem, this person could be a counselor, a helpline volunteer, or a religious leader at your place of worship.

3. Weigh the Pros and Cons of each Solution
    You can do this alone or recruit someone to help you. For each solution, ask yourself:

    -   How much time will it take me?
    -   How much money will it cost me?
    -   Will I need any outside help? Will it be easy for me to get this kind of help?
    -   Will I need any special equipment, training, or resources?
    -   Are there any important long-term consequences I should think about?

4. Choose the Best Solution
    If you're lucky, you'll have found a perfect solution. Unfortunately, in most cases, we have to compromise when solving problems. That's why writing out the pros and cons, as in the previous step, and talking to others is so important. Knowing that you have given the matter serious thought will make it easier to believe in your own judgment.

    Remind yourself that no one makes the right choices all the time. However, we can all try our best to work with the information and resources we have available at the time. Don't fall into the trap of postponing a decision just because you're afraid of getting it wrong.

5. Make a Plan
    Having found your solution, you now need to make a roadmap for the way ahead. Your goal is to draw up a step-by-step plan that leaves you feeling empowered rather than overwhelmed. Make each step as specific as possible.

    For example, suppose your goal is to sell your house and move to a new town. One of your first steps is to find out how much your property is worth. It would be more helpful to write, "Schedule a valuation within the next 7 days," rather than "Find out how much I could get for my house."

6. Execute your Plan
    Start with the first step and go from there. Take it slow and steady. Even people who aren't depressed need to be patient and encouraging with themselves when solving problems. You might need to break your steps down further. No step is too small as long as it moves you further toward your goal.
    Other strategies that might help:

    •   Planning a small reward for every step you take
    •   Asking a friend or relative to give you some support
    •   Working on a step for just 10 minutes at a time
    •   Keeping a log of your progress so you can see how far you've come

7. Evaluate the Results
    You've reached the final stage on your problem-solving journey. You've implemented the solution. Did it work? If not, what could you do differently next time? Perhaps

something unexpected happened, or you didn't get hold of the information you needed. We can all try our best, but there are lots of things in life that are beyond our control.

Even if things didn't quite work out as you hoped, give yourself lots of praise. You tried something new, and that's something to celebrate. Remind yourself that problem-solving is a skill. Like all skills, it becomes easier with practice.

SUMMARY

- Behavioral Activation (BA) and problem-solving are two practical tools lots of people find helpful in overcoming their depression.
- BA involves identifying activities you used to enjoy and scheduling time in which to do them.
- It's normal to feel resistance when you try BA, but you need to just go ahead and do it anyway.
- Problem-solving reduces feelings of depression because it makes you feel more empowered to overcome whatever challenges life throws at you.

CHAPTER 4:

CBT FOR INSOMNIA

Some people find it impossible to switch off at the end of the day. They toss and turn all night, unable to relax and fall asleep. The next day, they feel cranky and lethargic. Others can get to sleep, but then wake up every couple of hours. Does this sound like you?

If a lack of sleep is causing you serious health problems, your doctor might prescribe you a sleeping aid. However, doctors are reluctant to prescribe them long-term because it's possible to become dependent on them. It's much better to use drug-free therapies instead.

Research has shown that around 75% of people with insomnia report much better sleep after undergoing CBT.[25] Specifically, CBT for insomnia, commonly referred to as CBT-I, helps you regain control over your sleep schedule. In this chapter, you'll learn how to use CBT-I techniques and enjoy more restful nights.

THE FOUR PILLARS OF CBT-I

These are the four steps you'll find in most CBT-I programs:

Step 1: Learn about Sleep & Insomnia
Step 2: Stimulus Control & Sleep Scheduling

Step 3: Challenge Your Thoughts about Sleep

Step 4: Learn How to Relax

Let's look at each step in more detail.

Step 1: Learn about Sleep & Insomnia

You don't need to become a sleep expert, but knowing the basics will help you understand how CBT-I works. It will also help you see that losing sleep isn't a disaster, which, in turn, will reduce your sleep anxiety.[26]

When we sleep, we move through two phases: Rapid Eye Movement (REM) sleep, and non-Rapid Eye Movement (non-REM) sleep. Normally, we fall asleep within 15 minutes and enter non-REM sleep. Your heart rate slows. Your blood pressure drops. You might make movements, but your muscles are relaxed. Your breathing and circulation get slower.

Forty-five minutes to an hour after falling asleep, you enter REM sleep. As the name suggests, your eyes make small, rapid movements even though they remain closed. We only dream during REM sleep. During non-REM sleep, your heart rate and blood pressure remain low, but during REM sleep, they go up and down.

Approximately 30-45 minutes later, you move back into non-REM sleep. Throughout the night, you cycle back and forth between the two states. Most people complete four to six cycles. Not everyone needs the same amount of sleep. You might have read that everyone needs eight hours, but this isn't true. Some of us do perfectly fine with six, while others can't function well unless they get 9, 10 or even 11.

You are more likely to wake up during the second half of

the night because humans sleep more lightly in the early hours of the morning.

If you don't get enough non-REM sleep, which is common in people who wake up throughout the night, you will feel tired and depleted the next day. You can think of non-REM sleep as an overnight charger that helps us stay alert during the day.

If you don't get enough non-REM sleep, you'll feel exhausted. Sleep quality is more important than sleep quantity. The goal of insomnia treatment is not just to help you get a reasonable amount of sleep, but also to stay asleep long enough to move through normal sleep cycles.[27]

WHY DO SOME OF US DEVELOP INSOMNIA? ARTHUR SPIELMAN'S "3 Ps" MODEL

In the 1980s, Dr. Art Spielman proposed that three things are working together when someone develops insomnia: predisposing factors, precipitating factors, and perpetuating factors.[28]

Predisposing Factors

Some people are naturally good sleepers, but not everyone is so lucky. Your genetic makeup and personal traits might be working against you. Having a family history of insomnia, being born with a hyper-sensitive arousal system, or having a natural tendency to worry all raise your risk of sleep problems.

Precipitating Factors

A bereavement, redundancy, or even positive stress like planning a wedding can all trigger unhealthy sleep patterns. Can you pinpoint when your symptoms started? Do you think there was a precipitating factor in your case?

Perpetuating Factors

These are habits, behaviors, and thoughts that keep insomnia going. For example, if you lie awake worrying about why you can't sleep, you'll find it hard to drift off. Because you find it hard to get to sleep, you'll start worrying again the next time you get into bed. To break the cycle, you need to change the way you think about sleep and improve your sleep-related behaviors.

Your insomnia may have been triggered by a precipitating factor, but you might still struggle to sleep well even when the crisis or stressful period has passed. This is because insomnia can become a learned response. It takes a conscious effort to re-learn the art of sleeping well.

Step 2: Stimulus Control & Sleep Scheduling

Now that you have a general understanding of sleep and why you might be especially vulnerable to insomnia, let's look at the practical steps you can take to manage the problem.

Sleep scheduling is a technique that makes sure you are tired at bedtime. It involves recording and changing how much time you spend in bed, when you go to bed at night, and when you get up in the morning.

Stimulus control teaches your brain to associate going to bed with falling asleep, making it easier to sleep within 15 minutes of turning in for the night.

Together, stimulus control and sleep scheduling increase the number of hours between the time you wake up in the morning and go to bed at night. They also improve your sleep efficiency, which is the amount of time you spend asleep relative to the amount of time you spend in bed.

First, you need to start a sleep log.

A sleep log doesn't have to be complicated. All you need to do is draw up a table that lets you record the following information:

- The date
- When you went to bed
- When you got up
- How many times you woke up in the night
- The overall quality of your sleep
- How you felt in the morning
- What you ate and drank in the three hours before going to bed
- Whether you took any naps during the day
- What medications you took during the day, and when

Record your sleep for five days. Think of this as a fact-finding mission. You can then start to use the tips and techniques below.

How to schedule your sleep:

1. Choose a waking up time and stick to it every day.
   This is the first step in establishing a healthy sleeping pattern.

2. Choose a new bedtime based on how much sleep you are actually getting.
   Look at your sleep log. How many hours do you sleep per night? Add on one hour and count back from your waking up time as appropriate. This is your new bedtime. The goal here is to minimize the amount of time you lie awake in bed.

3. Limit your naps.

    Do not nap past 3 p.m., and do not nap for longer than 45 minutes, no matter how tired you feel. Napping later in the day will make it harder to sleep at night.

    After a few days, your sleep efficiency will improve. When you go to bed, you'll feel tired and ready for sleep. You can then start to increase the amount of time you spend in bed asleep based on how you feel during the day. For example, if you still feel tired when you are getting six hours of sleep per night, schedule another hour in bed and aim for seven hours instead. Remember, we all have different sleep needs.

STIMULUS CONTROL

1. Do not use your bed for anything other than sleep and sex. Do not watch TV, read, study, or have any emotional conversations with your partner. Your bedroom should be a peaceful sanctuary.

2. Get up within 20-30 minutes of waking.

    This conditions you to see your bed as a place to sleep, not a place to worry or plan the day ahead.

3. Go to bed only when you feel drowsy.

    Learn the difference between fatigue and sleepiness. Fatigue is a general sense of tiredness. When you are fatigued, you feel as though you need a rest. Sleepiness is the sensation that you could drift off at any moment. You should go to bed and turn out the lights when you feel sleepy, not just tired. Trust your body's signals instead of going by the clock.

4. Never stay in bed if you can't get to sleep.

If you can't fall asleep, or if you wake up in the night and can't doze off again, get up. Do something relaxing, such as a craft or reading a light-hearted book. Stay out of bed for a minimum of half an hour. When you start to feel sleepy, go back to bed. The golden rule: the longer you lie awake in bed, the harder it will be to get back to sleep.[29]

Once you have found a good routine, it won't matter if you occasionally sleep in or have a late night as long as you get back on track quickly.

More Tips for Better Sleep

1. Fix your diet
   Sugar, alcohol, and caffeine are detrimental to sleep. Sugar and caffeine are stimulants and will make it hard to fall asleep.

   Alcohol is a depressant. In theory, this should mean that it helps you relax. However, when the effects wear off, your brain and body will become more alert and you may wake up.

2. Time your workouts carefully
   Exercise is great, but working out in the evening makes it harder to fall asleep. Allow at least two hours between exercising and going to bed.

3. Fix your environment
   It's hard to sleep in a room that's too cold or too warm. According to the National Sleep Foundation, the ideal room temperature for sleeping is 60-67 degrees Fahrenheit.[30]

Step 3: Challenge Your Thoughts About Sleep

The next step is to challenge and restructure your thoughts about sleep. When you lie awake worrying about having insomnia, your insomnia will only get worse. When you worry, your body releases stress hormones, which stimulate your nervous system. Cognitive restructuring gets you out of this trap.

Here are some destructive thoughts, plus a reality check for each:

Thought: "I'll never manage to improve my sleeping patterns!"

Reality: CBT-I has been effective for many people. It can help you too. Within a few weeks, you'll be sleeping much better at night. Your mood will improve, and you will look forward to bedtime rather than dread it.

Thought: "If I don't get at least eight hours of sleep every night, my health will suffer."

Reality: It's true that chronic insomnia does increase your risk of some illnesses. The good news is that you can lower your risk easily by trying the techniques in this chapter. What's more, you may not even need eight hours of sleep. Anywhere from 6-11 hours of sleep per night is normal.

Thought: "I'm such a failure, I can't even get to sleep at night."

Reality: Insomnia is very common. Yes, falling asleep is a basic human function, but lots of people struggle to get enough sleep.

Thought: "I need drugs to fall asleep."

Reality: During times of crisis, such as sudden bereavement, your doctor might prescribe some medication to help you sleep.

However, most medical professionals don't think that drugs are the best way to cure insomnia. CBT-I is a safe, well-established method that works for most people who try it. Perhaps you are in the minority who need medication to sleep, but why not try CBT before going to your doctor? You might be surprised by how well it works.

Thought: "Unless I get a good night's sleep, I won't be able to function at work."

Reality: It's true that you're more likely to make mistakes after a poor night of sleep, but this doesn't mean you won't be able to function. You've probably made it through a day at work or caring for your children before, and you can do it again. Sometimes, the stress of worrying about your insomnia can make you feel worse than the insomnia itself.

Research shows that people with insomnia underestimate how much sleep they get, and overestimate how long it takes to get to sleep. Insomnia is definitely a problem, but your case might not be quite as severe as you think.[31]

When these beliefs creep up on you, ask yourself these questions:

- Is there any evidence this belief is objectively true?
- What is the evidence against this belief?
- Does holding this belief hurt or help me?
- What would I say to a friend in this situation?

Step 4: Learn How to Relax

If you're having trouble sleeping, you probably have symptoms of stress, anxiety, and depression too. The other chapters in this book are full of practical CBT exercises and tips to help you feel better, which in turn will improve your sleep.

A specific type of relaxation exercise, Progressive Muscle Relaxation (PMR), is popular with CBT-I therapists. If you practice it regularly, you'll be able to enter a state of relaxation whenever you like. This is helpful when you want to relax before bed, or if you want to get back to sleep after waking up in the middle of the night.

Exercise: Progressive Muscle Relaxation

1. Lie down in bed and close your eyes.

2. Breathe in. As you inhale, scrunch your toes. Squeeze the muscles as hard as you can. Hold this position for a few seconds.

3. Exhale. Relax your muscles.

4. Inhale and tense the muscles in your calves. Hold for a few seconds, then release and exhale.

5. Continue this pattern—inhale and tense, exhale and release—with all your major muscle groups. Finish with your facial muscles.

6. Repeat the exercise if desired. For best results, do it every day.

WORRY TIME

Everything seems worse at night. Lying in bed worrying is miserable and counterproductive. It certainly won't help you sleep. However, as you know, it's not that easy to stop feeling anxious. If you could decide not to worry anymore, you would have done so long ago.

"Worry Time" can help limit your worries. Pick a 20-30-minute time slot each day. During that time, let yourself feel as anxious or as worried as you like. If you start worrying at other times of the day—or in bed—tell yourself, "I'll save that for my Worry Time."

Caution!

If you have a sleep disorder or another illness, CBT-I might not be right for you. It's best to check with your doctor before trying self-help methods for insomnia. For example, if you have Restless Leg Syndrome (RLS) or another condition that causes your body to move in uncontrolled ways, you might need medication or physical therapy along with CBT-I.

Finally, remember that CBT-I will take time to work. You should expect that it will take at least 6 weeks to overcome your sleep problems.

SUMMARY

- Insomnia is a common problem.
- CBT-I is a special form of CBT designed to improve sleep patterns.
- CBT-I entails learning about sleep and insomnia, stimulus control and sleep scheduling, cognitive restructuring, and learning to relax.
- CBT-I can take a few weeks to work and requires patience.
- If you suspect you have a serious sleep disorder or have an illness that affects your sleep, consult a doctor before trying the strategies in this chapter.

CHAPTER 5:

CBT FOR ANXIETY

Everyone experiences anxiety from time to time. We all know what it's like to feel uneasy or to dread something. Anxiety can be mild, moderate, or severe.

Anxiety can be unpleasant, but it's healthy in small doses. If our ancestors never felt anxious about getting enough food or other issues of survival, we wouldn't be here today. Anxiety motivates us to act.[32]

Unfortunately, excessive anxiety can make life difficult. If your anxiety has taken over your life, it's time to make some changes. In this chapter, you'll learn about the most common types of anxiety, and how CBT can help tame your worries.

NOT ALL ANXIETY IS THE SAME

Anxiety comes in many forms, including:[33]

Panic disorder: A condition characterized by multiple, recurrent panic attacks. A panic attack usually starts suddenly and lasts for around 5-20 minutes. Symptoms include sweating, ringing in the ears, trembling, dizziness, nausea, shortness of breath, a choking sensation, palpitations, and tingling fingers.

You might also have disturbing, racing thoughts. You may think that you are going crazy, that you are about to die, or that the attack will never end. Panic attacks happen when your body releases stress hormones, including adrenaline. Adrenaline stimulates your nervous system, which explains the strange, frightening symptoms.

Phobias: An irrational or extreme fear of a situation, object, or animal. When someone encounters the thing they fear, they may have a panic attack.

Agoraphobia: An extreme fear of being stuck in a situation where it would be difficult to escape. An agoraphobic person might be scared of leaving their home, traveling on public transport, or visiting crowded places.

Generalized anxiety disorder (GAD): A condition in which someone finds themselves worrying about a wide range of events and situations. They feel worried most of the time and find it hard to relax. Even if one of their worries is resolved, they quickly move on to worry about something else.

Social anxiety disorder (SAD): A fear of social situations. Someone with SAD will worry or panic about going to parties, going to work, meeting people they don't know, and making small talk. If you have SAD, you probably spend a lot of time worrying about what others will think of you.

These conditions can look different, but they are all centered around feelings of anxiety. The exercises in this chapter can be helpful for anyone who has, or thinks they have, an anxiety disorder. Remember, you can't diagnose yourself with a mental illness. It's best to see a doctor or therapist who can make a proper assessment.

Exercise: How Does Anxiety Limit Your Life?

Working on anxiety is scary. You will need to move beyond your comfort zone and embrace the things that frighten you. To keep yourself motivated, take a moment to write down how anxiety limits your life and why you want to get better. How will things look when you are no longer afraid?

USING COGNITIVE RESTRUCTURING SKILLS TO OVERCOME ANXIETY

To gain control over your fears, you need to work on overcoming beliefs that fuel your anxiety and beliefs about anxiety itself.

Cognitive restructuring works well for people with anxiety. We already covered how it works in earlier chapters, but here's a quick refresher:

- Cognitive restructuring consists of three steps: Identifying your negative thoughts, weighing up the evidence for and against each thought, and then replacing unhelpful thoughts with a more constructive perspective.
- Asking thoughtful questions helps you take a rational approach.

When challenging a thought, ask yourself the following:

- What would I say to someone else in this situation?
- If I didn't feel depressed or anxious, how would I look at the situation?
- How would someone who isn't depressed or anxious look at the situation?
- Is there any objective evidence that my thought is true?

Cognitive Restructuring: What Are Your Beliefs about Anxiety?

As you know, beliefs feel very convincing in the moment, especially if you've been relying on them for a long time. But if you want to improve your anxiety, you've got to let them go. This exercise is the first step.

Exercise: Sentence Completion – What Are Your Beliefs About Anxiety?

Complete these sentences:
If I worry all the time, I'll...
If I didn't worry, I would...
When I realize how much time I spend worrying, I think...
Worrying makes me feel...
I first started having anxiety problems when...

When you completed the exercise above, did any of these beliefs come up?

1. "If I worry all the time, I'll keep myself safe."
   It's true that remaining vigilant can, in some cases, help you identify dangerous situations early. But worrying can't protect you from everything that could go wrong. If you think about the real calamities that have happened in your life, you'll probably realize that worrying would not have prevented them from happening. Most of the time, worrying is a waste of your energy.

2. "If I worry about the worst-case scenario, I won't be so upset or disappointed when it happens."
   Worry cannot protect you from loss or disappointment, and it can't keep bad things from happening.

3. "It's bad for me to worry so much."

   Worry can't make you go mad. Neither can you die from it. Sure, anxiety can be scary, but it won't kill you.

4. "I'm a born worrier. I'll never be able to get over my anxiety."

   Some of us do tend to worry more than others. That's just a fact of life. But we can all choose to face our fears and fix our thinking errors. There's a good reason CBT is so popular with therapists working with anxious clients.

ANXIETY & LOGICAL ERRORS

You already know that thinking errors can make depression worse. The same applies to anxiety.

Exercise: Logical Errors & Anxiety

Go back to the chapter on CBT and depression. In that chapter, we looked at how logical errors keep depression going. Which of these errors do you think fuels your anxiety? Why? Can you give specific examples?

Here are a few examples of the logical errors often seen in anxiety disorders:

Mind reading

Example: Andy has social anxiety disorder (SAD). He assumes that he "just knows" what other people are thinking. When he has to sit next to someone he doesn't know at his sister's wedding, he tells himself that they think he's boring and stupid.

Catastrophizing

Example: Maria gets very anxious about making mistakes at work. She turns in a project at work, and then worries that her boss will think it's no good. Her boss sends her an email, asking for a few minor adjustments. Maria's mind goes into overdrive. She assumes that her boss thinks she is incompetent, and that it's only a matter of time before she gets fired.

Over-generalizing

Example: Tom has to give a speech at work. It goes okay, but it could have gone better. He missed a couple of his presentation slides, and he knows he spoke too quietly. Instead of thinking about how he could do better next time, Tom tells himself, "I'm terrible at public speaking! I always mess up my presentations!" Tom then spends a lot of time worrying about going to work.

Labeling

Example: Sally has a fear of dogs. One day, she is taking a walk through the local park. She sees a large dog run away from its owner and knock over a small child. Although the child is un-hurt, Sally immediately decides that the park is dangerous. This makes her more likely to avoid the park in the future because she has told herself that it is unsafe.

Challenging your thoughts is the first step to recovery. Next, you need to follow it up with action! In the next section, we'll look at the cycle that keeps anxiety going.

BREAKING THE AVOIDANCE-ANXIETY CYCLE[34]

If something makes you feel afraid, your natural impulse is to remove yourself from the situation. In most cases, this is a good strategy. For instance, if an angry dog is running toward you, it makes perfect sense to move in the opposite direction as quickly as possible.

Unfortunately, changing your behavior so you don't have to face the things that make you anxious can backfire. This is known as avoidance. For example, if you develop a fear of public transport, you may start walking to work instead of taking the bus.

This kind of behavior works in the short-term. However, if you get into the habit of avoiding any situations that make you feel anxious, you'll never get the chance to see that everything can work out okay. Instead, you'll become trapped in a cycle:

- You avoid the thing that's making you feel scared.
- By doing this, you are teaching yourself that whatever you are avoiding really is something you should be afraid of.
- You keep avoiding it.
- You never get the chance to learn that it isn't so scary after all.
- You may also start to fear similar situations.
- Your life becomes increasingly limited, and your confidence starts to shrink.

To get past your anxiety, you need to confront your fears and learn that you can come out well on the other side. This is called "exposure therapy."

FACING YOUR FEARS USING EXPOSURE THERAPY[35]

In brief, exposure therapy works like this:

1. You pin down what, exactly, is making you anxious.

2. You make a list of specific situations that make you feel anxious or afraid.

3. You put these situations in a hierarchy, starting with the least scary situation.

4. You schedule your exposure, then follow through.

5. You expose yourself to whatever makes you feel anxious until you learn that you can survive the fear.

Exposure therapy is simple but difficult. It's easy to see how it works in principle, but putting it into practice requires courage.

If you are ready to give it a try, start with this exercise:

Exercise: Putting Your Fear into Words

In a single sentence, summarize the main source of your fears. For example, "I am afraid of speaking to people I don't know," "I am afraid of cats," or "I am afraid of visiting the dentist." This exercise gives you a starting point for your therapy and focuses your mind.

Having figured out your root fear, you can start to put together a plan of action.

Exercise: Make A Fear Ladder

Following the steps above, make your own "fear ladder." Try to think of 5-10 situations. Be precise. For example, if you are afraid of elevators, are you scared of elevators in department stores, office buildings, or other settings? Are you scared of traveling one floor, three floors, or from top to bottom of a building?

Here's an example of what a fear ladder might look like for someone with social anxiety who has a fear of talking to people in social settings. The first item on the list causes them the least amount of distress, whereas #10 is the scariest.

Social Anxiety Fear Ladder:

1. Saying "Good morning" to a colleague or neighbor
2. Asking a colleague or acquaintance whether they had a good weekend
3. Asking a shop assistant for help or advice
4. Making small talk with a friendly cashier or barista in a shop or café
5. Making a phone call to an old friend
6. Eating lunch with a colleague
7. Inviting two people out for drinks after work
8. Holding a small dinner party with four people
9. Joining a new hobby group or local club and attending the first meeting alone
10. Giving a presentation at work

Everyone's fear ladder will be different. This is just an example to show you what it might look like in practice.

SCHEDULING EXPOSURE

Don't let yourself procrastinate. The sooner you start, the better. If you are going through a crisis or major transition right now, such as relocating or starting a new job, you might want to wait until things have settled down before you start therapy. On the other hand, life rarely stands still, so don't wait until everything is perfect.

It's impossible to predict how long it will take for you to move past your fear. It depends on how strong your anxiety is, how much time you can spare to expose yourself to each step on your ladder, and how motivated you are to change.

Start by scheduling your first exposure session in your diary. Treat it with the same respect as any other appointment. Your time is precious, and this investment in your mental health is priceless. If you tend to procrastinate, ask a friend to hold you accountable.

When you are facing your fear:

1. Be patient
   Don't try to skip ahead. Only move up your anxiety ladder when you have conquered the first step, then the second, and so on. Be prepared to repeat each step around 5-7 times.

2. Give yourself enough time to wait for your anxiety to subside
   The human body can't remain in a state of panic forever. Panic attacks usually last around 20-30 minutes, then subside as the 'fight or flight' response wears off. It's possible to have multiple attacks, but it's not likely. Even if you are one of the unlucky few who feel panicked for a long time, your attacks won't hurt you.[36]

3. Do not use safety behaviors or distractions while waiting for your anxiety levels to drop
   Talking to someone, repeating mantras in your head, or holding a safety object are all distractions from the task at hand—facing your fear.

Exercise: Monitoring Anxiety Levels

Every time you expose yourself to a situation that makes you anxious, give yourself an anxiety score before and after each attempt. For instance, you may give yourself a score of 9 before putting yourself in an anxiety-inducing situation, and a 5 afterward. Your goal is to lower your anxiety to a score of 0-2. It's okay if this takes longer than you might like!

4. Reward yourself

Every step up your fear hierarchy is a cause for celebration. Give yourself frequent rewards, and praise yourself. Few people are brave enough to conquer their anxieties. You are doing great!

HANDLING PANIC ATTACKS

Panic attacks are the main symptom of panic disorder, but anyone can have them. They can be triggered by an event or a thought. Sometimes, there isn't a clear cause.

The good news is that, when you understand what's going on in your body and mind when you panic, you'll be well-equipped to deal with them.

When you notice the symptoms of an attack, your thoughts might go into overdrive. For example, when your heart speeds up, you might start thinking, "My heart is about to explode!" If you feel light-headed, you might think, "I'm going to faint!"

Your symptoms are caused by your body's natural fear response. During an attack, your body releases a cocktail of hormones and neurotransmitters, including adrenaline. It's an automatic reaction, honed by evolution. It's out of your conscious control.[37]

However, you do have a choice when it comes to interpreting your symptoms. For example, you can choose to think that your heart palpitations mean you are having a heart attack, but you can also choose to challenge this thought. You can choose to tell yourself, "This feels awful, but I am not having a heart attack. It's the adrenaline that makes me feel this way. It will be over soon."

Your thoughts can make the difference between an unpleasant panic attack and an attack that seems to go on forever and leaves you feeling traumatized. It all comes down to how you think about it.

Panic attacks are also linked to avoidance and safety behaviors, which keep anxiety going. Here's an example. You go to a shopping mall. You notice that it's very crowded. You think, "I might never find my way out if there's a fire!" You start to worry. Your body responds by releasing adrenaline and other hormones, which causes symptoms of panic. You notice that your heart is beating very fast. You think, "I'm having a heart attack!" You leave the mall as soon as possible. You sit outside the mall, feeling terrified, and vow never to go back in there again. The mere thought of returning to the mall makes you feel scared, and you start avoiding it.

The solution is to notice that you are having an attack, practice thinking helpful thoughts, and to give yourself the chance to see that the situation really isn't so bad after all. That means not fleeing, but instead waiting until the symptoms subside. This isn't easy. It's a form of exposure therapy. You need to stick it out and prove that panic attacks aren't the end of the world.

Here are a few typical thought traps people fall into, paired with some more realistic, balanced thoughts:

Thought: "I can't cope with this!"

Alternative thought: "I've had panic attacks before, and things turned out all right."

Thought: "I'm dying."

Alternative thought: "This attack won't kill me. It's my body's natural fear responses that are making me feel like this."

Thought: "I've got to get out of this situation right now."

Alternative thought: "I am safe. I need to stay in this situation to prove that things are all right."

> Thought: "I'll never stop having panic attacks. They are ruining my life."

Alternative thought: "Lots of people overcome their panic attacks. I can too!"

> Thought: "I'll never be able to cope with this unless I get some medication."

Alternative thought: "Drugs can only ever be a quick fix. I can learn to cope with these attacks by myself."

SYMPTOM PROVOCATION: PROVING YOU CAN COPE WITH WORRYING SENSATIONS

Symptom provocation is another form of exposure therapy. It involves deliberately triggering the same symptoms you get when you are having a panic attack, so you can see for yourself that they are harmless. It's also known as "interoceptive exposure."[38]

The most popular exercise is deliberate hyperventilation. When you hyperventilate, you breathe more quickly than usual. The levels of oxygen in your bloodstream go up, which triggers lots of the symptoms associated with panic, including light-headedness, tingling, and shortness of breath.

If you want to try this, find somewhere quiet and private where you can be alone for at least 10 minutes. Sit down in a comfortable chair. Take a few deep breaths. Gradually speed up your breathing until you start to experience the same symptoms you get during a panic attack.

Observe your symptoms for a couple of minutes. Watch as they subside. Practice this exercise a few times per week, and the thought of having a panic attack will no longer seem quite so terrifying.

If you don't want to try inducing hyperventilation, you can try spinning around on a desk chair for a few minutes to induce feelings of dizziness and light-headedness. If you want to replicate the sensations of a pounding heart or sweating you might experience during a panic attack, run up and down the stairs a few times.

Caution!

You can try symptom provocation by yourself, but if you start experiencing any physical sensations that are new or particularly worrisome, stop. It may be best to work through these exercises with a trained therapist.

WHAT ABOUT RELAPSES?

Lots of people have a few lapses when they've finished treatment for anxiety. It's totally normal. For example, someone who used to have social anxiety might suddenly find themselves worrying about an upcoming family party. You're more likely to have a relapse if you've been feeling tired or stressed.[39]

The answer? First, take good care of yourself. Eat a good diet, schedule time for relaxation, and talk to someone you trust when life feels overwhelming. Second, start using your favorite CBT exercises again. If you've used CBT to feel better before, you can do it again. You have every reason to be optimistic. CBT worked for you in the past, and it will work again this time around.

SUMMARY

- Anxiety comes in many forms, including panic disorder and agoraphobia.
- Avoidance behaviors and beliefs about anxiety can keep you trapped in anxiety cycles.
- Challenging these beliefs is the first step to overcoming anxiety.
- Exposure therapy is a structured framework for conquering your fears. The only way to overcome a fear is by confronting it until your anxiety peaks and subsides.
- Panic attacks are unpleasant, but you can deal with them by accepting the symptoms and changing how you think about them.
- Symptom provocation lets you see for yourself that panic attack symptoms won't hurt you.
- Relapse is common, but you can always use your CBT skills whenever and wherever you need them.

CHAPTER 6:

USING CBT TO BEAT OCD & INTRUSIVE THOUGHTS

A t least 2% of the population suffer from Obsessive Compulsive Disorder, commonly abbreviated to OCD. As the name implies, people with the disorder have obsessions and compulsive behaviors. It occurs in both sexes and all age groups.[40]

Obsessions are unwanted, unpleasant thoughts that can be very scary. They might be words, images, or urges that seem to pop up randomly or in response to particular situations. Common obsessions include a fear of germs, a fear of saying something obscene in public, and intrusive violent images.

Compulsions are repetitive mental acts (such as counting to 100 or silently saying a prayer) or behavior carried out to relieve the feelings triggered by the obsessive thought. For instance, if you have OCD and your obsession relates to germs or cleanliness, your response to intrusive thoughts about germs might be to wash your hands several times.

WHAT CAUSES OCD?

Like most mental illnesses, OCD is caused by a mix of genetic and environmental factors. If you have a close relative with OCD, you are more likely than the average person to develop it yourself. Research has shown that brain chemistry could play a role. For instance, people with OCD typically have low levels of serotonin, a neurotransmitter, in their brains.[41]

Sometimes, OCD symptoms start after a major life event such as bereavement or job loss. Personality is also a factor. If you've always been a perfectionist, you are more vulnerable to OCD.

THE OCD CYCLE[42]

1. Trigger
   An unwanted, distressing and intrusive thought, urge, or image enters your mind.

2. Anxiety
   The thought, urge or image triggers feelings of anxiety.

3. Compulsion
   You feel compelled to carry out some kind of behavior or mental act to counteract your anxiety.

4. Temporary relief
   Your compulsive behavior or mental act helps you feel better, but soon the anxiety comes back. The cycle starts again.

You don't have to experience both obsessions and compulsions to have OCD, but most people with the condition get stuck in this kind of cycle.

Exercise: Understanding Your Cycle

Make a list of your obsessions, anxieties, and compulsive behaviors. How do they relate to one another? Draw up a diagram showing how your personal OCD cycle works.

Here are a few of the most common obsessions:

- An extreme fear of catching a disease or becoming contaminated in some way—for example by touching doorknobs or handrails; during a global pandemic, of course, this fear is justified
- Worrying that you will accidentally cause harm or damage to yourself or others—for example by failing to make sure that all the windows are locked before you go out
- Worrying about deliberately hurting yourself, strangers, or those you love—for example, you may have intrusive thoughts about stabbing your partner or strangling your children
- A strong urge to tidy up objects, to order them in a particular way, or arrange them so that they are symmetrical
- Worrying that you find people or groups of people sexually attractive—some people become obsessed with their sexual orientation and have intrusive thoughts of themselves with someone of the same sex

It can be hard to examine your thoughts. You might feel ashamed, crazy or dangerous. In fact, it's extremely rare for someone with OCD to act on their obsessions.

Obsessions trigger compulsions, such as:

- Checking doors and windows multiple times.
- Checking to be sure that electrical appliances are switched off before leaving the house.
- Repeating words or mantras, either aloud or silently.
- Counting things.
- Ordering things.
- Cleaning the body or objects.
- Deliberately thinking "good" or "neutral" thoughts to cancel out the intrusive thoughts.
- Asking others for reassurance, e.g. "Do you think I'd ever act on my thoughts?"
- Going to extreme lengths to avoid triggering situations.

OCD doesn't normally get better by itself. You need to tackle the thoughts and behaviors, breaking the cycle so that they no longer have such a hold on your life. You can do this by reducing the thoughts and behaviors you use to cope with your anxiety (such as handwashing or other rituals), and by taking a more realistic approach to your obsessive thoughts.

INTRUSIVE THOUGHTS ARE NORMAL – IT'S YOUR REACTION THAT MAKES THE DIFFERENCE

Most people have unpleasant, intrusive thoughts from time to time. It's unlikely you have had OCD all your life. Think back to what life was like before your symptoms started. You probably had strange, unwanted thoughts occasionally. The difference? Back then, you didn't pay them much, if any, attention.[43]

Exercise: Do Other People Have Intrusive Thoughts?

You'll need a trusted friend or relative for this exercise. Tell them that you've been reading about OCD and that most people have intrusive thoughts. Ask them if they've ever had weird, crazy, random thoughts that took them by surprise. They will almost certainly say "Yes." Knowing that wacky thoughts are normal can be reassuring.

Telling yourself not to have intrusive thoughts does not work. The more you tell yourself not to think about something, the more you'll think about it. You can't treat OCD by willing it away. Instead, you need to interrupt your responses to the thoughts and learn to tolerate anxiety.

Why Reassurance-Seeking Doesn't Work

When an intrusive thought pops up, it's natural to ask family and friends for reassurance. For example, if you have intrusive thoughts about harming your spouse, you might ask them questions like, "Do you think I'm a violent person?" or "Do you think I'd ever kill someone?"

Of course, your family and friends will say things like, "No, you're definitely not a murderer," or "No, you'd never hurt anyone."

What's the problem with reassurance-seeking? It doesn't work.[44] It might make you feel better for a few minutes or even a few days, but the thoughts will come back. If reassurance worked, people with OCD would be able to cure themselves on the spot, just by asking the right questions. Sadly, OCD doesn't work like that. To make matters worse, asking the same questions over and over again can put a strain on the relationship.

Research is another form of reassurance-seeking. For instance, if you keep having obsessive thoughts that you will cheat on your partner and spend hours on the internet searching for signs that someone will have an affair, you are trying to reassure yourself. Even though you aren't talking to another person and asking their opinion, the same rule applies. It won't make you feel better. In fact, once you start researching a topic, you probably will fall down the internet rabbit hole and end up feeling worse.

You need to break the reassurance habit. Tell your loved ones that it's important you stop asking them to reassure you. If you ask them anyway, they need to say something like, "We agreed that I won't reassure you. Let's talk about something else."

If you use the internet for reassurance, you could:

- Block any websites you keep returning to.
- Use an app to limit your internet usage.
- Reward yourself for each day you manage to go without looking for reassurance online.
- Ask a friend to remind you to stay away from the internet.

WHY YOU NEED TO AVOID AVOIDANCE

Avoiding your triggers might work in the short term, but it isn't a cure. As you saw in the last chapter, avoidance isn't a good strategy for treating an anxiety disorder. It limits your life, makes you feel helpless, and fuels your worries. For example, let's imagine how an obsession with germs and cleanliness could lead to avoidance.

If someone feels anxious when they use a public bathroom because they fear contamination, they will try to avoid public bathrooms at all costs. The link between intrusive thoughts ("I'm going to be contaminated by germs!") becomes a compulsive behavior ("I'm not going anywhere near a public bathroom"). Every time they avoid public bathrooms, this link gets stronger.

The only way to break the chain is to keep yourself from responding to compulsive thoughts and learning to tolerate anxiety. Exposure and Response Prevention (ERP) is a popular CBT technique that teaches you to do just that.

Exposure and Response Prevention (ERP)[45]

In ERP, you allow your obsessive thoughts to surface and then face them without using compulsive behaviors. For instance, if you feel compelled to wash your hands three times after touching a doorknob, you would deliberately touch a doorknob but then abstain from washing your hands.

At first, ERP will be extremely difficult. It takes time to train yourself to avoid engaging in compulsive behavior whenever your anxiety is triggered. If you have had OCD for a long time, you may have already tried to avoid giving in to your behaviors. ERP requires a high level of commitment. You need to make a conscious choice—before your anxiety is triggered—that you won't follow your urges.

The good news is that ERP works fast. When you keep yourself from responding, you'll feel extremely anxious, but your anxiety will start to drop within 20 minutes. When you repeat this sequence several times, you'll start to become habituated. The anxiety will become more bearable, and your urge to carry out your old compulsions will start to fade. ERP can even become enjoyable because with every exposure you are triumphing over your old anxieties.

GETTING STARTED WITH ERP

You can use ERP as part of a self-help program, but you'll need to be well-prepared. If you expose yourself to your most feared situations too quickly, you may become overwhelmed and give up. You need to identify your triggers, then gradually work your way through the list.

Exercise: What Are Your Triggers?

Draw up a list of triggers. These are everyday situations that cause your obsessive thoughts to pop up. For instance, if you are afraid that you will harm an animal, seeing a dog might be a trigger. Rank your triggers in order, from the least to most scary. This will be the basis of your ERP ladder.

You can now start working your way up the ladder. If you have multiple obsessive fears, make a ladder for each. For example, if you have an obsessive fear about harming others and a fear of eating contaminated food, you will need two ladders.

Now, start scheduling your ERP sessions. You may need to expose yourself to a trigger several times before you can move past your fear. That's normal! Remember that your body can sustain a high level of anxiety only for so long.

RESISTING SUBTLE AVOIDANCE

Regular avoidance is easy to spot. Earlier in this chapter, we looked at the example of a person with a contamination obsession avoiding public bathrooms. However, not all avoidance is so obvious.[46]

Some people use other behaviors to manage their anxiety and avoid facing up to their fear. For example, they might be able to do something that scares them, but only if they can talk to someone else while they do it. Other forms of subtle avoidance include holding a comforting or "safe" object and deliberately thinking about other things. Be firm with yourself. Treat subtle avoidance just as you would more overt behaviors.

RESISTING URGES

If resisting an urge is causing you extreme anxiety, try reducing or delaying your compulsive behavior. For example, if you usually feel compelled to say a prayer whenever a "bad" thought of harming someone comes into your head, try to wait 2 minutes first.

Next time delay it by 5 minutes. Gradually increase the time until you learn that you can tolerate your anxiety and that nothing bad will happen if you don't give in to your compulsions.

MODELING

If you have been dealing with obsessions and compulsions for a long time, you may have forgotten what normal or typical behavior looks like. Ask a friend to show you how to do an everyday task that makes you anxious.

For example, if you feel an overwhelming compulsion to wash your hands multiple times after cleaning the bathroom, watch your friend clean and then wash their hands only once. Make sure you pick someone you trust. Don't choose someone who will become impatient or tease you about your compulsions.

IMAGINAL EXPOSURE (IE)[47]

If the thought of exposing yourself to your trigger situations is too overwhelming, you can use Imaginal Exposure (IE) first. IE entails imagining yourself in a situation that triggers your anxiety. By visualizing the scene and observing your anxiety come and go without using your compulsive behaviors, you can prepare yourself for full ERP.

For example, let's suppose you have an obsession with cleanliness and germs. Let's say you have constructed a written ERP ladder, and exposed yourself to a few triggering situations, but can't seem to get to the next step, which entails touching a door handle in a public bathroom.

Instead of going out and actually exposing yourself to the situation, you would sit quietly and visualize it. You would imagine how it would feel to touch the handle, and then observe any worrying thoughts and anxieties that pop up. You would then carry on visualizing the scenario until your anxiety subsides. Just like regular ERP, you might need several sessions before you start feeling okay about the situation.

It's important to note that using IE like this should be a warmup to ERP, not a substitute. IE is a way to desensitize yourself to anxiety before exposing yourself to real-life triggers.

KEEP AN EYE ON YOUR STRESS LEVELS

OCD tends to flare up when someone is under stress. If you have a big life event coming up, such as starting a new job or relocating, make sure you have healthy coping mechanisms in place. Otherwise, you might find yourself slipping back into old obsessive patterns. Simple self-care, such as getting enough sleep and spending enough time with friends and family, is important.

Summary

- OCD is an anxiety disorder. Sufferers get stuck in a cycle of obsession, anxiety, and compulsion.

- OCD does not get better on its own. You need to expose yourself to your triggers and practice resisting your urges.

- Exposure and Response Prevention (ERP) is a technique that teaches you to resist your usual compulsive behaviors.

- Resisting urges is a key skill that is difficult to master, but you can use a gradual approach if needed.

- Keeping your stress levels under control will help protect you from relapse.

CHAPTER 7:

USING CBT TO BEAT PROCRASTINATION

CBT is a great approach to treating mental illness, but it has many other applications. In this chapter, we're going to look at how you can use CBT techniques to overcome a common problem that holds lots of people back—procrastination.

WHAT IS PROCRASTINATION?

Procrastination is choosing to delay or not complete a task for no good reason, even though doing so will have negative consequences. Usually, procrastination involves doing something else that isn't as important, just to fill in the time or provide a distraction.[48]

You can think of procrastination as a bad habit that might affect several areas of your life, or you might only procrastinate in some situations. For example, you might be organized at work, yet procrastinate on DIY projects at home. It might feel as though you can only motivate yourself in some settings or when you are working for a paycheck.

WHY IS PROCRASTINATION SUCH A BIG DEAL?

Everyone procrastinates sometimes. It's human nature. If you can choose between a boring task and something less challenging, it's always tempting to pick the latter. Our brains have evolved to seek pleasure and avoid pain. Unpleasant tasks are psychologically uncomfortable, so our first instinct is to avoid them if possible. For 20% of the adult population, procrastination is a chronic problem.[49]

Unfortunately, as we all know, ignoring a task doesn't make it go away. Although distracting yourself with something easier and more fun works well in the short term, you'll still have to face reality at some point. To make matters worse, delaying a task makes it more stressful when you do finally get started.

It's common for a procrastinator to beat themselves up for not starting the job or task sooner. They may also get locked into a spiral of procrastination that looks something like this:[50]

- The procrastinator delays a task, which makes them less stressed in the short term.
- As the deadline looms, they realize they have increasingly little time in which to do the work, which makes them feel even more daunted about the task ahead.
- To make themselves feel calmer and less overwhelmed, they decide to delay the task yet again...
- ...but they have to acknowledge that the job needs to get done somehow. They then seek out further distractions, and the cycle begins again.

There's another dark side to procrastination—it damages your self-esteem. When you decide to do something but fail to follow through, you are sending a clear message to yourself: "I can't be trusted." If you can't trust yourself, it's hard to grow and maintain any self-respect.

Finally, procrastination can have serious consequences for your relationships. If you keep reassuring a loved one that you really will get around to doing XYZ but then never actually do it, they will start to resent you. Procrastination can also set your relationships back if you can't get around to making a decision. For example, if you procrastinate on deciding to have children, your partner may feel increasingly distressed as the months or years tick by.

Exercise: What Tasks Have You Been Procrastinating On?

Make a list of all those tasks you've been delaying. Why do you think you've been procrastinating? How long have you been putting them off—days, weeks, months, or even years? How has your procrastination affected your work? How has it affected your personal life?

ARE YOU MAKING EXCUSES?

Even if you don't think of yourself as a creative person, there's a good chance you are very accomplished at coming up with excuses for your procrastination.

Do any of the following sound familiar?

- "I work better under pressure anyway, so it doesn't matter if I delay it."
- "I'm too tired to do anything now. I'll start it tomorrow."
- "I need to feel inspired before I can do anything, so I'll start another time."
- "I'm not going to do very well on this project anyway, so why put too much effort into it?"

- "It's a lovely sunny day, I'd be silly to stay inside and work!"
- "Life's too short to work all the time, I deserve to enjoy myself."

These excuses are based on assumptions, such as:

- "I shouldn't have to do anything I don't like."
- "It's always better to have fun rather than get stuck into a boring task."
- "It doesn't matter how hard I try, I'll get it wrong anyway. What's the point?"
- "I need to wait until I want to do a task before sitting down to do it."

Excuses make you feel better about procrastinating, but they don't change the facts. You still have to do the task at some point, and procrastinating will just make you feel worse. Some of these excuses have a grain of truth, which makes them very compelling. For instance, it may be true that you feel tired, and that starting the task will require a lot of effort.

But—and this is an important idea to grasp—this doesn't change the fact that you need to start it anyway. In this chapter, you'll learn how to reason with your excuses and become more productive.

Exercise: Challenging Your Excuses & Assumptions

What was the last excuse you used? Ask yourself these questions:

- *What is the evidence that this excuse is valid?*
- *What assumptions am I making in this situation?*

- *What is the evidence to suggest that it would be better for me to start anyway?*
- *How would I feel if I started the task anyway?*
- *How would I feel if I delayed it even further?*
- *What would I say to a friend in this situation?*

Having answered these questions, what do you think your next course of action should be?

TOLERATING DISCOMFORT

Learning to tolerate discomfort and boredom is essential. When you possess the ability to keep going with a task even when you'd rather be doing almost anything else, you'll become an unstoppable productivity machine!

Whether or not we realize it, many of us believe that boredom is absolutely unacceptable. We live in a world where the internet, TV and other forms of entertainment are available at all hours of the day and night. No wonder we dislike the idea of being bored. But the harsh truth is that life is a mix of pleasure and pain, and the two go together. You need to let go of the assumption that life should be comfortable and that you shouldn't have to do anything that isn't immediately gratifying.

Exercise: Noticing Discomfort

The next time you want to abandon a task, take a deep breath and sit or stand still instead. Tune into your body. How do you feel? Do your muscles feel tense? How is your posture?

Are you prepared to keep working anyway? Acknowledge your feelings, and then continue with your task.

This is a powerful exercise because it challenges your assumption that it's best to give up whenever you feel like walking away. It won't take long for you to realize that discomfort is actually normal and bearable. Paradoxically, the better you are at accepting discomfort, the easier your work will be.

Getting through a dull task can bring a sense of achievement. It might not be fun, but it's definitely satisfying to discover that you could tackle that job after all. You don't have to pretend that a dull task is enjoyable, but you can take a moment to savor the satisfaction you'll get when it's complete.

GETTING OVER YOUR FEAR OF FAILURE

Do you procrastinate because you have an underlying fear of failure? You're not alone.[51] For many procrastinators, missing a deadline can feel safer and more manageable than turning an assignment in and receiving criticism.

To overcome this problem, you need to address your thoughts and feelings about failure.

Do any of these sound familiar? Let's look at a few destructive beliefs you might have about failure, and how to replace them with healthier thoughts.

1. "If I don't get it right, I'll never succeed."

   Have you ever watched a baby learn to walk or a young child learn how to write their name? No one is born with these skills; they must be learned through trial and error. You won't get everything right the first time, but this doesn't mean you will always get it wrong.

2. "I can't cope with negative feedback."

   Criticism is the end of the world when you're depressed

or have low self-esteem. However, when you are in a balanced frame of mind, it's just part of life.

Perhaps you have been on the receiving end of some scathing criticism before. But you're still here! That's proof that you can survive it. It's also worth remembering that not all feedback is constructive. You don't have to assume that the other person is correct.

3. "If I fail a test or get a low grade, it means I'm a total failure."

Failing in the past doesn't mean you are bound to fail in the future. Failure can be a great teacher. You can learn from your mistakes and do better next time around.

Exercise: Who Fails?

This exercise is divided into two parts.

First, think of a famous person who inspires you. Do a bit of online research. You'll almost certainly discover that they have failed at a few things!

Next, ask a trusted friend or family member if they've ever had a big setback that they've had to overcome. Again, you'll almost certainly learn that they've had to deal with failure.

WAITING FOR INSPIRATION

Lots of procrastinators assume that if they don't feel inspired, they shouldn't start a task. This is a dangerous assumption.[52]

You can't afford to wait around for inspiration or motivation to strike. Inspiration is fickle. Even great artists, writers, scientists, and other people who seem very engaged with their work don't rely on it. To be really successful, you need to work regardless of your mood. If you wait to feel inspired before beginning, especially if the task is dull, you could be waiting forever.

The same applies to feeling tired. Yes, it's harder to begin a job if you are fatigued. But that doesn't mean you can't or shouldn't start anyway. You'll be surprised by how much you can get done even if you aren't at your best.

GETTING OVER UNCERTAINTY

Another unhelpful assumption is that you have to know precisely what you are doing before you get started.

Yes, of course you need a sensible plan when you begin your work, but many tasks are open-ended. It's impossible to predict exactly what you'll need to do at every stage. It's best to put together a plan before you begin but remain flexible if you encounter a setback. If you hit a roadblock, you can draw on the problem-solving skills you learned earlier in this book. Try to reframe difficulties as a learning experience.

MORE PRACTICAL TIPS FOR BEATING PROCRASTINATION

1. Do the worst first
   Is there a task you are dreading? Get it out of the way, and you will find it easier to face the rest of the day. You'll also feel proud of yourself for taking charge of the situation.

2. Prioritize your tasks
   Common sense tells us that we should work on our most important tasks first, so spend a few minutes grading the items on your to-do list. For each task, ask yourself whether it is important, urgent, or both.

Work through your tasks in this order: Urgent and important, urgent and unimportant, non-urgent and important, and non-urgent and unimportant.

3. Break tasks down into small chunks
Take big projects step by step. Write down your final deadline, then break down the small tasks you need to accomplish between now and then. Keep breaking them down until you no longer feel overwhelmed. If it's a very big project, ask your supervisor or someone with more experience to check your plan to ensure it makes sense.

4. Build momentum
Can't find the energy to start a task? Do something you like for a few minutes, then dive into the task. The momentum can give you a jumpstart.

5. Keep a time log
Scheduling is much easier if you can confidently predict how long a task will take. Start keeping notes detailing how many minutes, hours, or days you need for each task. You can then refer to your notes when scheduling similar tasks in the future.

6. Set a timer and challenge yourself to work for five minutes
Five minutes is barely any time at all. You'll probably find that it isn't too hard to keep going when the timer goes off.

7. Use rewards
You deserve a reward for getting your tasks done. It doesn't have to be expensive. A magazine, a movie, a cup of coffee, or a long bath with your favorite bath oil are all good choices.

8. Make it easy to pick up a task again

   If you need to work on a task over several days, finish each session by setting yourself up for success when you pick it up again. For example, if you are writing a report, leave a couple of sentences half-finished.

9. Get an accountability buddy

   Tell a friend or colleague what you plan to achieve and when. Ask them to check in on you. You could take it further by placing a bet. For instance, you could bet your friend that you will have done Task X by Day Y, or you'll buy them lunch.[53]

Exercise: Three New Strategies

There are lots of practical tips in this chapter, but you'll get overwhelmed if you try to implement them all at once. Start by choosing three strategies you like and trying them out over the coming week. If they work for you, that's great! If they don't, stay open-minded and try something else. We all have different needs and working styles.

SUMMARY

- Procrastination is the act of putting off a task for no good reason and choosing to do something less important instead.

- Procrastination has serious consequences for your work and relationships.

- Procrastinators make a lot of excuses for their behavior. If you procrastinate, you need to identify these excuses and challenge the underlying assumptions.

- Practical solutions to procrastination include prioritization, doing the worst tasks first, and challenging yourself to work for a few minutes at a time.
- Learning to tolerate discomfort will improve your stamina and help you get boring jobs done.

CHAPTER 8:

RELEASING REGRET & GETTING OVER GUILT USING CBT

D o you ruminate about the mistakes you've made? Do you want to feel more comfortable with your past choices? In this chapter, we're going to look at how CBT can help you move past feelings of guilt. If you leave them unchecked, your regrets will hold you back from reaching your full potential.[54] It's time to reframe your past, learn from your mistakes, and work toward a brighter future.

How Do You Feel about Guilt?

Everyone makes mistakes. We all have our faults. Even the kindest, most patient, and most moral of us have made poor choices. Unfortunately, hurting other people is part of being human.

CBT gives you the tools to understand where guilt and regret come from, how to move past them, and how to avoid making bad choices in the future. Remember, how you react to events—including your mistakes—is just as important as the event itself.

YOU ARE NOT RESPONSIBLE FOR EVERYTHING

If you are prone to guilt and regret, you probably have a habit of assuming too much responsibility. When you are too quick to say, "Yes, this situation is entirely my fault!" your view becomes warped. In reality, most unfortunate events aren't caused by one person. Life is more complicated than that.

For example, let's say that your relationship has recently broken down. You and your partner have fallen into a pattern of getting into trivial fights that turn into screaming matches. To make matters worse, you disagree on a couple of other issues, including the question of marriage—you want to marry, and they don't.

So, who is at fault in this story? If it happened to a friend, you would probably reassure them that there are many factors at play. For example, you might tell them:

"Sometimes, relationships just don't work out."

"It sounds like you wanted different things. It hurts a lot right now, but it may be for the best that the two of you broke up."

"Neither of you are bad people, you're just incompatible."

You would not (hopefully!) say things like:

"This is all your fault. If you'd been nicer and compromised more, you'd still be together."

"The relationship ended because you are a bad communicator. Your partner never did anything wrong."

"This is your problem. You need to work on yourself more. If you'd spoken up about your problems earlier, you'd definitely still be together."

The strange and sad thing is that most of us have no trouble being kind and compassionate to our friends, but we are very harsh on ourselves. We often take a balanced view of someone else's situation, but then pile blame on ourselves whenever things go wrong in our own lives. This leads to guilt, regret, and a sense of hopelessness.

Slicing the Responsibility Pie[55]

The following exercise will help you step back from a problem or situation and understand the part you played in it.

Exercise: The Responsibility Pie

Make a list of everyone who played a role in the event you're feeling bad about, such as a breakup or a fight.

Now, draw a large circle on a piece of paper. This is your Responsibility Pie. Draw lines to divide this pie up into slices. Draw a slice for everyone on your list. Make the size of the pieces proportionate to their responsibility. Don't worry about getting the sizes or percentages exact. Go with your gut instinct.

Look at the pie and remind yourself that most life events have multiple causes. Yes, perhaps you should have made a different choice, but it's unlikely that the blame rests with you alone.

Yes, But What If It Really Was My Fault?

Of course, you might have made a big mistake, and no one else is to blame. For instance, let's say you go to a conference for work, get drunk, and cheat on your partner with a colleague who doesn't know you aren't single. Your partner finds out, and they end the relationship.

In this case, your partner isn't to blame. If you were to create a Responsibility Pie, the only name on there would be yours.

However, even when you have done something most people would consider wrong, it doesn't mean you need to feel guilty forever. Lots of us have beliefs about guilt that are untrue and unhelpful. By identifying and challenging them, you can put your guilt in its proper place, process it, and then move on.

Exercise: What Are Your Beliefs about Guilt?

Complete the sentences below:

> "If I didn't feel guilty, I would…"
> "I don't think I can give up my feelings of guilt because…"
> "Guilt is useful because…"

What do you think your answers reveal about your beliefs?

COMMON BELIEFS ABOUT GUILT & WHY THEY ARE SO DESTRUCTIVE

1. "If I feel guilty, I must have something to feel guilty about." This is simply untrue. For instance, some people feel guilty when they survive an accident in which others died. This kind of "survivor guilt" is clearly irrational. It's an example of emotional reasoning. Just because you think you are a bad person who should be ashamed of yourself doesn't mean you actually have anything to feel bad about. Only by stepping back and taking a long look at the situation can you really come to a reasonable conclusion.

2. "If I feel guilty, it means I am a bad person." Even if most people would agree that your guilt is justified, you are not a bad person. This line of thinking is an example of generalization, which is a cognitive distortion. Just like everyone else, you are a complex individual who has done great things but also made mistakes.

3. "Guilt will stop me from hurting people in the future."
Don't fall into the trap of assuming that guilt somehow
protects you from repeating your mistakes. You might
think, "Well, at least holding onto my guilt will make
me think twice before doing something wrong!"

This approach is doomed to fail because it undermines your self-confidence. Your morals and values are
better at helping you make good choices, not guilt. Guilt
also damages your relationships with other people. It
makes you negative and afraid, and your loved ones will
always have the sense that your decisions and emotions
are driven by something they can't see or understand.

Finally, guilt sucks up your energy. You end up wasting time beating yourself up instead of making positive
changes.[56]

4. "I need to feel guilty forever because I need to punish
myself for what I've done."

In small doses, guilt is healthy. It's a kind of warning
signal. Guilt lets you know that you've violated your
own moral code. When we feel guilty, we know it's time
to make amends and apologize if appropriate.

However, feeling guilty for a long time doesn't benefit anyone. If you've hurt someone else, they won't feel
better just because you feel bad. Yes, you can apologize,
but the mere fact that you're carrying around guilty
feelings won't make a difference. You cannot go back in
time and change the past.

Guilt becomes self-indulgent after a while. It doesn't
always feel like a punishment. In fact, it can become
almost comfortable. If you don't let go of your guilt,

you'll build a self-image as a "bad person." You need to take responsibility for your past, and how your feelings are keeping you stuck in place.[57]

It sounds counterintuitive, but this can actually make your life easier. After all, if you are a bad person, you are beyond hope and have nothing to offer this world. So why bother working hard or building better relationships? Clinging to your guilt gives you an excuse to be lazy.

5. "If I let myself stop feeling guilty, this means I approve of my own actions."

    Have you ever been reluctant to forgive someone because you don't want them to let them off the hook? The same principle can apply to your own guilt. On some level, you might think that allowing yourself to live guilt-free means that you are totally fine with the things you've done.

    It doesn't have to be this way. You can recognize when you've done something wrong, learn from it, and then move on. Releasing your guilt doesn't mean you approve of your own actions. It just means that you've decided not to give them too much time and attention.

6. "If I make a mistake, I am an unacceptable human being." This thought can be traced back to a single core belief: "I must be perfect, or I am worthless." This belief is both illogical and harmful. No one is perfect. The sooner you realize this, the happier you will be. You wouldn't expect your friends and family to behave impeccably at all times, would you?

7. "If I keep analyzing the situation long enough, I can work out exactly how much of the blame I deserve."

Some of us want to know precisely what went wrong in a situation that left us feeling guilty. Unfortunately, the world doesn't work like that. In most cases, there's no objective, scientific way to figure out exactly how much blame lies with us. It's smarter to invest your energy looking forward instead.

Do You Feel Guilty for Having Fun?

We all have the right to relax and have fun. In fact, taking time off from our responsibilities is important for our mental and physical health.[58]

Sadly, lots of us feel bad the moment we make time for ourselves. We tell ourselves not to be selfish, that we should be getting on with our chores, that we are lazy, and so forth. This is often a problem for parents, especially mothers, who are expected to put other people first.

Here are a few beliefs you might need to shake:

1. "Parents who want time alone are selfish."
   In reality, parents who want alone time are smart. Happier parents are more patient with their children.

2. "Putting yourself first makes you a bad person."
   It's not wrong to look out for your own interests. Helping others is great, but caring for yourself is a basic life skill too.

3. "Unless you are working all the time, you are being lazy."
   Most of us need to work to earn a living. Work also has other benefits, such as giving us a sense of purpose. However, we need to balance it with downtime.

4. "Enjoying yourself is a waste of time."

   Making good memories, either by yourself or with others, isn't a waste of time. What's more, some people have their best ideas when they are relaxed outside of working hours.

5. "It's bad to have a good time when other people can't join in."

   You are not responsible for everyone else's wellbeing. If someone else can't join in, perhaps because they don't have time or money to take part, that isn't your problem.

6. "You need to help other people solve their problems before you can relax."

   If you are a parent, you are of course responsible for keeping your children safe and meeting their needs. However, in general, there is nothing wrong with taking a break from solving everyone else's issues and focusing on yourself for a while.

Exercise: Scheduling Alone Time

Over the coming week, schedule at least one hour of alone time. You may need to get up earlier or go to bed later. If you work, you could get creative with your lunch hour. For example, you could schedule three 20-minute reading breaks throughout the week. No matter how busy your lifestyle, you need to take time for yourself. In fact, the busier your life, the more important it is!

If your family or friends try to make you feel guilty or ashamed for spending time alone, that isn't your problem. You may need to set boundaries. Explain that you—like everyone else—need a break from time to time, and you expect them to honor the time you set aside for yourself.

MAKING AMENDS

CBT is action-oriented, and CBT therapists encourage clients to make amends for their mistakes if possible. For instance, if you feel guilty because you lost your temper with a friend a few weeks ago and felt the issue wasn't resolved, you could call them up and apologize.

When you apologize, don't make it about yourself. Do not give excuses for your behavior or try to explain it away. Simply tell them that you are sorry, that you regret causing them hurt, and that you will never do it again. If they have any questions, answer them truthfully. If you don't understand the motives behind your own behavior, then say so.

Note that no one has to accept your apology. Sometimes, people feel that words are not enough. This is why you have to rely on yourself for closure; you won't always get it from someone else.

Don't be surprised if the other person tells you that you have nothing to worry about. You might find that you've blown the incident out of proportion. In fact, they may have forgotten about it altogether. This is humbling. It's a gentle reminder that the world doesn't revolve around you.

FEELING GUILTY WHEN THINGS GO WELL

So far, we've looked at the kind of guilt you might feel when something goes wrong. But what about the kind of guilt you feel when you realize how lucky you are?

For example, if you were born into a family with plenty of money and they supported you in getting a college education, you are probably in a far better position than someone born into poverty to parents who didn't care much about their prospects. Good fortune can make you feel guilty.

Exercise: What Does Good Luck Feel Like?

Imagine that tomorrow morning, you wake up to learn that you've won the lottery or inherited a huge sum of money from a relative you didn't even know existed. Give yourself a moment to really get into this fantasy. What are you seeing, hearing, thinking?

Now ask yourself these questions: How do you feel? After the initial shock has worn off, are there any other feelings mixed in with your happiness? Are all of them pleasant?

You may have heard about the 'just world' hypothesis and how many world events actually come down to luck. When you truly accept how many things in our lives come down to chance, you'll start to feel less guilty when you catch a break.

On a slightly more morbid note, remember that even the most privileged among us aren't protected from freak accidents, death, illness and relationship breakdowns. If your luck turns against you, you'll regret wasting time feeling bad about how good you have it now.

Finally, remember that feeling bad doesn't usually help others feel better. If you can let yourself enjoy your good fortune, then at least one person gets to be happy. Think back to the last time you went through a hard time in your life. Would you really have felt better if everyone else felt guilty because they weren't going through the same thing? Probably not!

WHEN TO GET FURTHER HELP

If you are finding it difficult to understand whether something really was your fault, or the event left you traumatized, it's time to seek professional help. This is because sorting out what happened can be upsetting and confusing after abuse or trauma.

Summary

- Guilt and regret are normal feelings, but they can be destructive if you cling to them for too long.

- Creating a Responsibility Pie lets you own your role in a situation, and then move on.

- If you hold unhelpful beliefs about guilt, you will spend a lot of time feeling regretful unless you work on letting them go.

- Make amends to people you have hurt if possible, but don't expect closure. No one has to accept your apologies.

- We all have our share of good and bad luck. There is no reason to feel guilty when things go well.

CHAPTER 9:

HOW CBT CAN HELP YOU BEAT ADDICTION

One in three people is addicted to at least one substance or behavior. You can become addicted to anything that gives you pleasure or a feeling of reward. Drugs, alcohol, nicotine, and gambling are the most common. Other addictions include shopping, using the internet, and work.[59]

SIGNS YOU HAVE AN ADDICTION

You might be addicted to a substance or behavior if:[60]

- It's having a negative effect on your day-to-day life.
- You've tried to stop or cut down but haven't succeeded.
- You get withdrawal symptoms when you try to stop.
- You are willing to engage in risky behaviors to get more of the substance or to engage in the behavior.
- You've lost interest in your old hobbies.
- You are ashamed of your behavior.
- You've stopped caring about your appearance.

How Do Addictions Develop?

Addiction begins when you experience a rush of pleasure or a "high" after using a substance or engaging in a behavior. Our brains are very good at working out what makes us feel good, and so we start to crave it again in the future. The more often you use a substance or behavior, the stronger the habit becomes.

When you are addicted to something, you suffer withdrawal symptoms when you attempt to stop. For example, if you are addicted to online gaming and try to stay away from the internet for 24 hours, you might feel agitated and preoccupied with gaming. It might be hard to focus on anything else. If you are addicted to alcohol, you might suffer tremors and headaches when you try to stop drinking.

The quickest and easiest way to stop these symptoms is to give in to your cravings. This makes you feel better for a while but keeps the cycle of addiction going.

Several risk factors can make you more vulnerable to addiction.[61] Psychologists think there is a genetic component to addictive behaviors. An addiction can also be a coping mechanism. If someone has suffered a bereavement, lost their job, or has an untreated mental illness, addiction can provide a distraction. Spending time with others who have addictions also puts you at risk because seeing others abuse substances or engage in addictive behaviors makes it seem normal.

Caution!

CBT isn't always enough to cure an addiction. If you are addicted to a substance, you might need other forms of help, such as supervised detox or medication that helps you cope with the physical effects of withdrawal. If your addiction has damaged your relationships, you and your loved ones may need therapy to rebuild trust.

How Do CBT Therapists Treat Addiction?

CBT for addiction is usually given as a structured program. Treatment is normally broken down into these stages:

Stage 1: Assessment
Stage 2: Behavioral Change
Stage 3: Cognitive Change
Stage 4: Relapse Prevention

Every recovery program is different, but most feature these components.

Stage 1: Assessment

In addiction therapy, assessment is made up of "The 5 Ws."[62]

Ask yourself the following:

When?

At what times of the day or night do you engage in addictive behavior? Do you find it harder to control your addiction on weekdays or weekends?

Where?

Where do you buy substances, or where do you engage in addictive behavior? For example, do you drink more when you visit a friend's house or compulsively use the internet when you are alone in your bedroom?

Why?

What compels you to use a substance or engage in addictive behavior? Are there any internal or external cues that seem to come up again and again? For example, do you start to crave alcohol whenever you feel anxious?

With/from whom?

Who, if anyone, is normally around when you act on your cravings? Do you have any friends, acquaintances, or relatives with the same addiction? When you're together, does your addiction feel normal?

What happens?

What feelings do you get when you act on your cravings? Do you get a sense of pleasure, relaxation or something else? Do you feel distressed by your behavior and, if so, why?

These questions are designed to give you an insight into your personal patterns of addictive behavior.

Exercise: Behavior Record

Draw up a table with the following headings: Situation, Thought, Feelings, Behavior, and Consequence. The next time you act on a craving, make notes under each heading. Complete as many records as you can over the coming week.

In time, you'll start to notice that your behaviors follow one or more patterns. For instance, you might notice that you tend to go online to play games immediately after coming home from a stressful day at the office, and then suddenly it's past midnight and you've been so involved in your game that you haven't eaten dinner. Your partner is mad because you haven't paid them any attention, and you know you'll be tired at work the next morning.

In this case, the situation would be, "Coming home from the office." Your thought might be, "I need to unwind." Your feelings could be described as, "I'm really stressed and just want a distraction." Your behavior would be, "Spent all night on the computer." Finally, the consequences would be, "Felt tired, missed dinner, argued with my partner."

Stage 2: Behavior Change

Answering the 5 Ws and keeping behavior records will help you discover your triggers. These are situations, people, and feelings that you associate with addictive behaviors. The more often you engage in a behavior following exposure to a situation, the more powerful that trigger will become.

Triggers can be internal or external. Internal triggers include mood states, such as stress, anxiety, excitement or fatigue. External triggers include vacations, payday, and spending time with people who also engage in addictive behaviors.[63]

In summary, triggers and cravings work like this: You encounter a trigger (e.g. a bar), which causes a thought (e.g. "I could get a drink"), which leads to a craving (e.g. for alcohol), which leads to addictive behavior (e.g. drinking).

If a situation involves triggers, a therapist will class it as a high-risk situation. A key part of CBT for addiction is to consciously decide to decrease the amount of time you spend in these situations. Instead, you need to increase the time you spend in low-risk situations, i.e. those that don't trigger you.

When you've identified your triggers, the next step is arranging your schedule so you avoid them.

Here are a few tips:

1. Work out how much time your addiction currently takes up and choose activities that will fill the spare time completely. The less time you have to dwell on your addiction, the better.

2. Choose activities that are totally incompatible with your trigger situations. For instance, do not join a hobby group that meets near a mall if you are trying to overcome a shopping addiction.

3. Try to find hobbies and interests that genuinely excite you. Addictive behaviors give your brain a big jolt of pleasure. You might have to try a few new activities before you find one that fills the void.

4. Reward yourself every time you pick a healthy activity over spending time in a high-risk situation.

5. Spend time with people who aren't struggling with an addiction. You need to spend time with individuals who lead balanced lives and don't depend on compulsive behaviors to have a good time.

Exercise: Avoiding Triggering Situations

How can you plan to avoid triggering situations? What could you do instead? Set yourself a challenge: Over the coming week, replace at least two triggering situations with low-risk activities instead.

Stage 3: Cognitive Change

The way you think about your addiction can make just as much of a difference as how you manage your triggers.[64] Unhelpful beliefs about addiction and craving will hold you back. Look at the core beliefs below:

Belief: "If I have a craving, that means I'm going to give in."

Reality: It's hard to believe when you're in the grip of a craving, but you don't have to act on your urges. Cravings can indeed feel very compelling, but if you can teach yourself that giving in isn't inevitable, you'll discover that you can resist them.

Belief: "I can't cope with my cravings."

Reality: Overcoming addiction is tough. But people can and do recover. They aren't injured or killed by their cravings. They get through them and keep making strides toward recovery. You can do the same.

Belief: "If I have a relapse and give in to a craving, that means all the days I've spent free from addictive behavior don't count."

Reality: A lapse doesn't undo all your good work. This is a classic example of "all or nothing" thinking. A healthier way to look at the situation is to congratulate yourself for your recent progress, remind yourself why you want to quit your addiction, and then proceed as best you can.

Belief: "If I have a lapse, it means I'll never be able to quit. I'm doomed to stay an addict forever."

Reality: You have a choice after a lapse. You can indulge in "doom and gloom" thinking, which will only make you feel worse. Or you can look at the situation, try to learn from it, and vow to do better next time.

Belief: "I can have just one drink/visit one store/spend just one hour at the casino."

Reality: Your brain and actions influence one another. Every time you act on a craving, you are reinforcing addictive behavior, which will lead to further cravings in the future.

Take a moment to review the evidence for and against this thought. Is it really true that you can have "just one"? When you tried to moderate your behavior in the past, what happened? Be honest with yourself.

PRACTICAL TIPS FOR HANDLING CRAVINGS

1. Surf the urge
    When you feel the beginnings of a craving, don't try to push it away. Pause, take a deep breath, and tune into your body. Do you feel tense? Jittery? Cravings don't last forever; they peak and then subside.[65] Tell yourself that you can observe the craving and wait it out.

2. Acknowledge and talk about the craving
    Telling someone how you feel can make a craving feel less scary. Phone or text a friend and describe how you feel.

3. Thought stopping
    Picture a big red STOP sign whenever you notice un-helpful thoughts creeping in. For example, if you catch yourself thinking, "I need a cigarette to unwind, it's been a long day," imagine the STOP sign popping up and blocking the thought.

4. Distraction

   Choose a distraction and immerse yourself in it for half an hour. Pick something that will hold your attention. If it involves practical work or exercise, so much the better. Good distractions include playing music, reading or writing in a journal, going for a brisk walk, and deep-cleaning the bathroom.

5. Positive self-talk and affirmations

   Remember, challenging your thoughts and replacing them with more helpful cognitions is a big part of CBT. When a craving hits, remind yourself that:

   You are trying your best

   You've already made progress by identifying your cravings;

   You'll feel very proud of yourself when the craving passes and you haven't acted on your urges.

Stage 4: Relapse Prevention

It's normal to have lapses when recovering from an addiction.[66] A lapse is a brief slip-up. For example, if you have a gambling addiction, buying a scratch card or playing online poker one evening would be a lapse.

Lapses can be discouraging, but they don't necessarily mean you are spiraling back into full addiction. As long as you frame your lapse as a slight setback, instead of a complete disaster, you can quickly get back on track.

Use positive self-talk. Instead of telling yourself that you are a failure, remind yourself that the road to abstinence is often bumpy. Instead of telling yourself that you'll always be an addict, remind yourself that most people can, and do, recover.

Learning How To Say "No"

Social situations and people can be a big trigger. To conquer your addiction, you need to work out how you will handle high-risk social interactions and maintain your abstinence.[67]

Practice what you will say the next time someone offers you a substance or encourages you to act on a craving. Write down your responses and rehearse them in front of a mirror. Good responses are short, memorable, and assertive.

For example:

"No, thank you, I don't drink."

"I don't smoke."

"No, thank you, I've quit."

"No, thank you, I don't do that anymore."

Make eye contact, and use a firm, even tone of voice. Some people don't take the hint the first time, so you might have to repeat yourself.

"Friends" Who Make You Feel Bad Aren't Your Friends

A friend is someone who wants the best for you. Anyone who tries to stand in the way of your sobriety or tempts you to engage in addictive behaviors is not your friend. People who respect you will respect your boundaries. If they have an addiction of their own, it's their choice to continue, but they have no right to belittle you.

Later in this book, you'll discover how CBT techniques can make you more assertive. However, being assertive won't change other people. Some addicts find that, in order to change their lives for the better, they need to form healthier friendships.

SUMMARY

- It's possible to be addicted to anything that makes you feel good.
- If you are addicted to something, both your work and personal life probably will suffer.
- CBT helps people overcome addiction by giving them a framework to identify triggers, change their behaviors, think about their addiction in a new way, and to prevent relapse.
- Addictions are personal, but they also have a social component. To stay abstinent, you might need to develop new friendships.

CHAPTER 10:

USING CBT TO OVERCOME JEALOUSY

CBT is most often used for treating mental illness and stress, but it can benefit anyone struggling from problems many of us face, including relationship issues. In this chapter, you're going to learn how to handle jealousy.

JEALOUSY IN RELATIONSHIPS

Do you worry that your partner is cheating on you, even if you don't have any evidence? Are you always watching them when you're out in public in case they are checking out other men or women?

A little jealousy in a relationship is normal and can even be healthy.[68] Jealousy keeps us vigilant. If you feel slightly jealous when your partner starts flirting with someone else, that's normal. The trouble starts when you let jealousy destroy your peace of mind, or when you start fighting with your partner despite having no proof that they are betraying you.

Jealousy can become a self-fulfilling prophecy. Jealousy is usually based in a fear of loss.[69] Unfortunately, your jealous behaviors can push your partner away. For example, if you suspect that your partner is being unfaithful and start questioning them about their feelings for their friends or colleagues, they will quite rightly become annoyed and resentful. They may also start to pull away from you or label you "crazy" or "paranoid." Jealousy is unattractive, and someone with healthy self-esteem won't want to stay with a jealous or possessive partner.

So, what can you do about jealous tendencies? CBT can help. Just like any other feeling, jealousy is associated with a set of thoughts and assumptions. Identifying and challenging your thoughts is the first step to a more realistic approach to your relationship.

Is Your Jealousy Productive or Unproductive?

Productive jealousy is useful. It points out where things have gone wrong in a relationship. It gives you a starting point for change. For example, let's say you are jealous because your partner spends lots of time with their best friend on the weekend. Your jealousy could encourage you to have an honest conversation with your partner in which you say you'd like more attention.

Unproductive jealousy doesn't prompt useful change, just worry and rumination. If you are dwelling on something that you have no control over, such as the possibility that your partner is flirting with a work colleague, you have a choice to make. You can either leave the relationship, learn to work with your jealousy, or stay with your partner until both of you become unhappy.

Working with Unproductive Jealousy[70]

Just like anxiety and depression, jealousy has cognitive and be-havioral components. When you understand how they fit to-gether, you can find a way through your feelings. The key is self-acceptance, plus a willingness to step back and see your thoughts from a new perspective.

The next time you get caught up in jealousy, ask yourself these questions:

1. Am I using emotional reasoning?
   Jealous people think that, because they feel jealous, there must be a good reason for their worry. This isn't true. You can still feel jealous even if your partner hasn't done anything wrong. Imagine your partner suddenly started accusing you of cheating. Assuming you've been faithful, their feelings wouldn't change the facts. Therefore, we can see that feelings aren't always a reliable guide.

2. Am I assuming that jealous thinking is protecting me?
   No one can keep their partner from cheating or looking at other people just by worrying about it. Ultimately, it's up to both parties to stay faithful. Realizing this can be quite liberating. You aren't responsible for your partner's behavior, only for how you respond.

3. What will these feelings of jealousy cost me?
   We've already established that jealousy isn't attractive. Imagine that you never overcame your jealousy. Close your eyes and imagine what would happen in your relationship. Picture your partner's exasperated face as they try to reason with you or tell you that they've had enough and are leaving.

4. What underlying beliefs are fueling my jealousy?
   Jealousy is often rooted in a feeling that you aren't good enough.[71] People who value themselves don't live in fear that their partners will leave the moment a more

attractive person comes along. If you are jealous, and there's no logical reason behind your feelings, it's time to take a close look at your self-esteem.

Do any of these sound familiar?

"I'm not very attractive or interesting."

"I can't make it on my own."

"People always betray me, so I need to look out for myself."

"If my partner left me, no one would ever want to date me."

It's important to be honest with yourself here because you will never move past your jealousy unless you tackle them.

Exercise: How Do Your Thoughts Set You Up for Jealousy?
When you read through the list above, did any thoughts jump out at you? Where do you think these thoughts came from? Have they always been a problem for you, or did something happen (such as infidelity in a past relationship) to make you think this way?

When you develop a more positive self-image, you will feel less jealous. You will realize that you are worthy of a supportive relationship with a faithful partner and that you don't need someone else's validation to feel good about yourself.

The following exercise is a thought experiment that will help you realize that you can cope with infidelity or the end of a relationship. This is a powerful exercise because, when you acknowledge that the end of your relationship wouldn't be the end of the world, you won't feel so distressed by the thought of your partner cheating. As a result, jealous thoughts will lose some of their hold on you.

Exercise: Picturing the Worst

Close your eyes and imagine that your jealous thoughts were proved true. For example, if you worry that your partner is cheating on you, imagine coming home one day and discovering them in bed with someone else. What can you see and hear? How are you feeling?

Now, imagine that the relationship has ended, and you are alone. What would you do next? Picture yourself picking up your life and slowly starting again, perhaps in a new home or with a new group of friends. Picture yourself feeling and working through your emotions.

This exercise isn't enjoyable, but if you repeat it regularly, the thought of your partner cheating on you won't seem quite so terrible. Of course, betrayal is immensely painful, but this kind of visualization will help you see that you can handle the worst if it should happen.

LEARNING TO TOLERATE UNCERTAINTY

No one can predict the future. Unless you spend every hour with your partner and take away their phone, it's possible that they will cheat on you. Sure, some people are much more likely to be faithful than others, but anyone can stray. On a morbid note, everyone will die eventually. We can't choose whether our partners go first, and there's no way of knowing exactly how many years we have left.

Your relationships will feel much more relaxed when you learn to live with uncertainty. Later in this book, you'll pick up a few techniques to help you live mindfully in the present moment.

Forgive yourself for feeling jealous. Berating yourself for feeling jealous won't benefit you or your partner. Although it's your responsibility to handle your feelings, it's unrealistic to shut down all jealousy forever. It's something you'll live with all your life—but it does get easier.

ENVY & UNHELPFUL COMPARISONS

Envy is fine in small doses. Just like romantic jealousy, it can even be helpful. It can give you valuable clues about what you would like to achieve, which, in turn, can give you a sense of direction.

For example, if you don't have a graduate degree and feel envious whenever a friend or relative earns a Masters degree, it might be a good idea to start thinking about going back to school. Or if you've been thinking about starting a fitness regimen, seeing photos of other people looking healthy and happy can be a source of positive inspiration.

However, if you spend a lot of time feeling envious of others, your self-esteem and relationships will start to suffer. Even if you are a good actor, your friends, colleagues, or family will realize that you envy them. Your body language and tone of voice will give you away eventually. They might begin to feel uncomfortable talking about themselves, which will weaken your relationships.

So, what can you do when envy strikes? Here's a step-by-step guide to help you feel better quickly:

1. Acknowledge how you feel.
    Take a deep breath and identify your feelings. If you are alone, say them aloud. If you like journaling, write them down.

2. Identify what you think the comparison says about you. Next, tap into your core beliefs. For instance, let's say you are envious because a friend has recently earned a promotion. Once the initial feeling of envy has passed, perhaps you start to think, "I'm stuck in my career. I'll never get the job I want. I'm too stupid, and I'm not ambitious enough."

3. Challenge the thought.
   Are your thoughts really accurate? To continue the example above, do you know with 100% certainty that you'll always be stuck in a job you hate? Is it really true that you are stupid? What do you gain by holding onto this thought? What would you tell a friend in the same situation?

4. Ask yourself whether you are idealizing someone else's body or life.
   By focusing on only one part of someone, you are dehumanizing them. That doesn't matter too much if you will never meet them, but it can be damaging if they are a friend or colleague. Would you feel frustrated if someone else reduced you to a single achievement? You're more complex than that, and so is the person who triggered your envy.

5. Draw on your problem-solving skills.
   If you want to make a significant change in your life, reframe your envy as a reason to pull out your problem-solving skills and make a plan for how you can meet your goals. For example, if you are frequently envious of your friends' relationships, make plans to start meeting new people.

Exercise: Who Really Has a Perfect Life?

Have you ever envied someone who later turned out to be struggling with serious problems? Perhaps they had relationship problems, health problems, or other troubles they were hiding from you or the rest of the world?

Now flip it around—what do you hide from the world? Perhaps you are a very open person who shares all of their problems, but most people edit their lives to make them seem happier and less chaotic than they are in reality.

This exercise is a reminder that no one is perfectly happy or successful all the time. As the saying goes, assumptions are dangerous things to make! Wouldn't you feel silly if you wasted time envying someone, only to later discover they are secretly struggling with lots of personal problems?

THE BEST FIX FOR ENVY

When you value yourself, other peoples' successes aren't a threat. You can admire and congratulate them without feeling jealous, and even feel happy on their behalf. People who accept themselves know that worth isn't a zero-sum game. Everyone is equally worthy as a human being, whatever their circumstances in life.

Exercise: Why Are You Awesome?

You'll need to work with a trusted friend or family member during this exercise. Ask them to help you make a list of your best qualities. You can do this alone, but it's often hard to see ourselves as we really are, so getting a second opinion makes the exercise more powerful.

Next to each trait, write down three pieces of evidence. For instance, if you regularly help your elderly neighbor with their shopping, that would be strong evidence that you are kind and caring.

Read through the list and evidence when you need a boost. To get the most from it, add extra traits and evidence whenever possible.

Self-appreciation is a powerful skill. It not only helps you cope with envy and jealousy but bolsters you against depression. What's more, people who value themselves are more attractive. If you want to attract a partner, appreciating yourself is a great first step.

SUMMARY

- Jealousy in a relationship can be healthy in small amounts, but unproductive jealousy can be destructive.
- Challenging your underlying beliefs about jealousy and yourself will help you feel better.
- Realizing that you could cope with a relationship ending is empowering.
- No one can predict the future; it is always possible that your partner may leave. Accepting this will help you come to terms with jealousy.
- Envy is normal, but you need to keep it in check. Otherwise, it can make you unhappy and damage your relationships.
- Acknowledging your feelings and identifying unhelpful thoughts, together with self-appreciation and problem-solving, can conquer envy.

CHAPTER 11:

BECOMING MORE ASSERTIVE & COPING WITH CRITICISM

In a healthy relationship, both people can talk about their needs, and they can give and receive constructive criticism without feeling threatened or rejected.

Unfortunately, many of us aren't very good at telling our partners when we would like to change something in our relationship. We might worry that they will resent us, or maybe we just don't know how to start a conversation without getting whiny or angry.

What's more, we may find it hard to process criticism, even if it's loving and carefully worded. Anything other than acceptance and praise can feel like a major threat.[72]

This is where assertiveness training comes in. When you behave assertively, you stand up for your wants and needs while respecting your partner and the relationship. But assertiveness goes beyond behavior. It's about adopting a specific mindset that will help you communicate with anyone and develop healthy relationships based on mutual respect.

In this chapter, you'll discover how to stand up for yourself and assert your rights in a relationship. You'll also discover how to handle criticism so you can learn and grow from feedback.

So, What Does It Mean To Be Assertive?

To understand what assertive behavior is, you can compare and contrast it with passive, aggressive, and passive-aggressive behavior:[73]

Passive behavior: Passive people put others' needs before their own. They do what they are told. When someone tells them that their needs or opinions are wrong, passive people don't fight back.

When passive people receive criticism, they automatically agree and change their behavior in an attempt to please the other person. They rarely stop to consider whether the feedback is helpful or true. In fact, most passive people tend to have low self-esteem, and so they agree with anyone who says they have messed up, or even that they are a terrible person.

Here are some typical beliefs you might have if you're a passive communicator:

"Other people know more than I do, so I should listen to them."

"If someone criticizes me, it means I am a bad person."

"My ideas and thoughts are probably wrong, so I shouldn't share them."

"It's arrogant and rude to stand up for your own needs."

Aggressive behavior: Aggressive people believe that their desires should come first. If they believe someone is trying to get in the way of their wants or needs, they will lash out. Aggressive people aren't always violent. They may use verbal aggression instead or launch a campaign of emotional abuse.

When an aggressive person is criticized, they either dismiss the feedback immediately or become angry. They see criticism as an insult and a threat to their ego.

Here are some typical beliefs you might have if you're an aggressive communicator:

"Other people should listen to me because my opinions and needs are more important than theirs."

"Being angry is the only way to get respect."

"Attack is the best form of defense."

"As long as I protect myself, it doesn't matter what other people think."

Passive-aggressive behavior: Passive-aggressive people may appear compliant on the surface, but their behavior makes it clear that they aren't happy with the situation. They might resort to sabotage as a form of revenge, or just to make it clear how unhappy they are. For instance, a passive-aggressive person might agree to take on a task they don't want to do, but then do such a bad job that no one asks them to do it again.

A passive-aggressive person may not agree when someone criticizes them. If they don't agree with a piece of criticism, they might say so—but in a sarcastic, snide or subtly dismissive way. Alternatively, they might appear to agree with a piece of critical feedback, but then deliberately ignore it.

Here are some typical beliefs you might have if you're a passive-aggressive communicator:

"Confrontation is bad, so I have to use sneaky tactics to get my own way."

"It's unsafe to stand up for myself."

"Other people can't be trusted."

"Other people can't tell me what to do."

Assertive behavior: An assertive person tries to balance their needs with those of others. They know they won't always get what they want, but they believe in standing up for their rights. They make themselves heard, without resorting to intimidation tactics.

When an assertive person receives criticism or negative feedback, they evaluate whether it's true or helpful before responding. They may or may not act on criticism, depending on the source and whether they think it's true. Either way, assertive people have robust self-esteem that can't be damaged by negative feedback.

Here are some typical beliefs you might have if you're an assertive communicator:

"I'm important and worthy in my own right—and so is everyone else."

"I can handle difficult conversations."

"My self-worth doesn't depend on what anyone else thinks."

"If someone hurts me, I can get over it. I'm strong."

So, how can you become more assertive? First, you need to identify any mental blocks you might have about asserting your rights. Second, you need to master some practical techniques that will rapidly improve your communication skills.

Exercise: What Kind of Communicator are You?

Based on the descriptions above, how would you describe your communication style? Some of us are a mix of two styles. You might use different styles depending on who you're talking to. For example, you might find it easy to be assertive at work but slip into a passive communication style when arguing with your partner.

CHALLENGE YOUR BELIEFS ABOUT ASSERTIVENESS

How do you feel when you picture yourself as an assertive person? Nervous, hypocritical, anxious? Lots of us carry around unhelpful beliefs about what it means to be assertive.[74] Unless you take a close look at these beliefs, it will be hard to make progress. Here are a few of the most common negative beliefs, along with more helpful alternative thoughts:

> *Belief: "Being assertive means being a bully."*

> Alternative thought: "Bullies are not assertive, they are aggressive. Being assertive is about striking the right balance between standing up for your own rights and respecting other peoples' wishes."

> *Belief: "If I'm assertive, I'll drive everyone away."*

> Alternative thought: "Confident, friendly people will respect me if I'm assertive."

> *Belief: "It's not very ladylike to be assertive."*

> Alternative thought: "Women and girls are taught from an early age that it's unfeminine to be assertive, but it's actually good to be an assertive woman. Assertive women get what they need and want in life."

Belief: "It's OK for others to be assertive, but my own needs don't matter."

Alternative thought: "Everyone has basic needs. Everyone has the right to be heard and to be respected. That includes me."

Belief: "Unless I take a 'tough love' approach with others, they won't respect me. They'll walk all over me."

Alternative thought: "Assertive people are usually more respected than angry, aggressive people. True, being aggressive might help me get my own way, but it will damage my relationships. Assertive communication is just as effective—and everyone else will probably like me more, not less."

Practical Tips To Become More Assertive

1. Start saying "No" more often.

    Are you a people-pleaser? Do you tend to go along with what everyone else wants, only to feel resentful later? The only solution is to learn how to decline requests and invitations.[75] For example, let's suppose your sister wants you to babysit her children on Friday, even though you know you'll be tired at the end of the working week.

    Instead of gritting your teeth and saying "Yes," you could use one of the following assertive responses instead:

    "No, I can't, I'll be too tired. I hope you find another solution."

    "Thank you for asking me. You know I like spending time with your kids. But I've got to say 'No' this time because I'll be too tired."

    "No, I'm not available that night."

Practice by saying "No" to low-level requests. For example, if your friend asks you to lend them a small amount of money, you could say, "No, I can't do that. I need to save whatever I can." "No" is a complete answer in its own right. If someone doesn't respect a "No," that's not your fault—they need to learn to respect other peoples' boundaries.

2. Use "I" statements.[76]

    "You" statements can sound accusatory, which isn't helpful if you are in a tense situation. Try to start sentences with "I need," "I feel," or "I would like" instead.

    Keep statements simple and to the point. For example:

    "I need to leave by 6 o'clock."
    "This will cost $1,200."

These are examples of "simple assertion." "I" statements are also useful for explaining how you feel. For example:

    "I feel angry."
    "I feel worried."

You can extend "I" statements to show empathy with someone else's position while still asserting your own needs.

For example:

    "I understand that you don't like having dinner earlier in the evening, but until I get settled into my new job, I'd like you to accept that this is the routine for the foreseeable future."

"I know that you don't like taking phone calls in the evening, but I'd like to get your feedback on an urgent matter."

3. Watch your body language.

   Your posture and voice make a big difference in how you feel about yourself, and how others see you. Keep your arms and legs uncrossed, sit or stand up straight, and keep your shoulders relaxed. Keep your tone of voice even. Never shout. If you appear calm and assertive, others will take you more seriously.

4. Use the broken record technique when someone tries to override you.

   If someone tries to overload you with objections and irrelevant arguments, rephrase and repeat your original response. Persistent people may ask you the same question several times, but even the rudest individuals will get the message eventually if you stand by your answer. Don't allow yourself to be sidetracked.

5. Find an assertiveness role model.

   CBT therapists sometimes tell their clients to find a role model if they are trying to change their behavior. Do you know someone who is assertive without being aggressive? Watch them carefully and see what you can learn.

6. Focus on behavior, not character, when asking someone to behave differently.

   If you want to ask someone else to change their behavior, use this formula:
   • State their observable behavior.
   • Tell them how it affects you.

- Tell them how this makes you feel.
- Tell them how you would prefer them to act in the future.

Here's an example of the formula in action:

"When you don't pick up ingredients for dinner on your way home when you promise to do so, it means I have to go and get them myself, come home, then make the evening meal. This makes me feel tired and disrespected. In the future, I'd like you to either pick up the ingredients or let me know in plenty of time if it won't be possible."

7. Spell out consequences.

    If you have tried asking someone to change their behavior but to no avail, the next step is to assert consequences. This is only appropriate as a last resort, and only when you are in a position to impose punishments or sanctions. Never make empty threats; the other person may see through them or decide to call your bluff.[77]

    Stay calm, keep to the point, and remain civil.

For example:

> "By failing to sign in when you arrive at work for the third time this week, you are violating an important company protocol. If you do this again, I will have to initiate a formal disciplinary procedure."

> "I have asked you to tidy your bedroom, and you have not done it. If you don't do it by tomorrow, I will confiscate your phone over the weekend."

You Have the Right to Put Your Safety First

Don't force yourself to be assertive if doing so would be un-safe. If someone is behaving in an abusive way, or you have a good reason to think they will become very angry if you assert yourself, it's best to excuse yourself from the situation as soon as possible.

Exercise: Role Playing

Role plays are a safe, effective way to practice your assertiveness skills. Ask someone you trust to play the role of someone who tends to make unreasonable requests. Repeat the role-play several times until you feel confident that you could say "No" in real life. You may wish to start by thinking of a recent example of a time you had trouble declining a request. Re-enact the scene. What could you have done differently?

How to Handle Criticism

No one is perfect. We all receive criticism from time to time. It isn't much fun to hear someone highlight your shortcomings, but criticism can be helpful. If you can accept feedback and act on it, you'll make more progress in your career, studies, and even personal life than people who block out criticism or become overly defensive.

Exercise: How Do You Normally Deal with Criticism?

When was the last time someone criticized you? Did you make the most of the feedback by changing your behavior, or did you try to block it out? Take a moment to think about how your response to criticism might be holding you back from fulfilling your potential.

8 STEPS TO HANDLING CRITICISM

1. Remind yourself that criticism doesn't determine your self-worth.

    You are a valuable and worthy human being, regardless of what anyone may say about you. Even if you have made a mistake, this doesn't mean you are a bad person. When you remember this, criticism won't seem quite so threatening.

2. Take a deep breath and wait a moment before reacting. Give yourself a moment to process what the other person has said. It's better to pause for a few moments, or even to take a few minutes alone, than say or do something you regret.

3. Consider the source.

    Not all criticism is created equal. Do not assume that it is true or justified. Feedback can be completely accurate and fair, or total nonsense. Most of the time, it's somewhere in between. Avoid 'all or nothing' thinking. Be prepared to take to heart the criticism that makes sense and dismiss the rest if it's irrelevant or given out of spite.

    Talk to a person you trust if you find it hard to differentiate between constructive and destructive criticism.[78] They will be able to help you take a step back and assess the situation.

4. Ask clarifying questions if the other person is being vague.

    If someone gives you a piece of general negative feedback, ask for more information. Some people are not good at communicating what they mean, so you have to put some effort into finding out what they are trying to say.

For example, if someone tells you, "I suppose you'll find it hard to complete this project because you aren't very organized," ask them, "In what ways do you think I'm not very organized?"

5. Try to focus on the words, not the tone.
Some people lack self-awareness and communication skills and may not know how to keep their tone of voice steady. Keep your focus on what they are saying, not how they are saying it.

6. Defuse the criticism if it's destructive, inaccurate or unfair.
You can agree with criticism in part, agree in principle, or agree in probability. The best option depends on the situation and the other person's temperament, but all three techniques work in the same way. They take the sting out of the criticism and lessen the other person's hold on you.[79]

First, you can agree in part. If the criticism is partly correct, pick out the relevant details and repeat it back to the other person. This lets you defuse the situation without validating the rest of their feedback.

Criticism: "You're lazy. You never help around the house, you didn't pick up the dry cleaning, and you hardly ever walk the dog."

Response: "You're right in saying that I do rarely walk the dog."

Alternatively, if the other person's logic is correct but their criticism is flawed, you could agree in principle.

Criticism: "You aren't using the right software for compiling this report. It has lots of security bugs. We'll lose our most important data."

Response: "True, if there are security bugs then we could lose some data."

Finally, you agree in probability. This involves acknowledging that, in theory, something could come to pass. However, it doesn't mean you have to agree with the criticism in its entirety.

Criticism: "If you don't start keeping to a strict budget, you won't be able to meet your basic expenses. You'll be broke by next year."

Response: "You're right, I could run out of money."

7. Apologize if necessary.
   If you have made a mistake, own up to it. Make apologies or amends as appropriate.

8. Decide on an action plan and share it if appropriate.
   If the criticism is fair, explain what you will do differently in the future. Be specific. For instance, if your boss has criticized your public speaking ability, you could tell them about the speaking course you intend to take.

   Finally, reward yourself! As you've probably noticed, not many people are good at working with criticism. If you can master this skill, your performance at work will improve, you'll gain a reputation as a calm, reasonable person, and your self-respect will blossom.

SUMMARY

- Being assertive doesn't come naturally to many people. Many of us are held back by our beliefs about what being assertive really means.
- There are four main types of communication styles: passive, passive-aggressive, aggressive, and assertive.

- Using "I" statements, monitoring your body language, and learning how to say "No" are key steps in learning to be more assertive.

- Roleplaying exercises will help you practice assertiveness skills.

- Dealing with criticism can be tough, but you can learn to accept it, defuse it if necessary, then use it as a tool for growth.

CHAPTER 12:

CBT & MINDFULNESS

O ver the past decade, mindfulness has become increasingly popular in the world of psychology. Mindfulness-Based Cognitive Therapy (MBCT) combines some of the principles of classic CBT along with breathing exercises, meditation, and mindful practices that help you accept reality exactly as it is.

In this chapter, you'll learn what mindfulness is, why it's proven to be such a powerful tool, how it's inspired a new kind of therapy, and how you can use mindfulness exercises to improve your psychological wellbeing.

WHAT IS MINDFULNESS?

Mindfulness is simply the act of paying attention. When you are in a mindful state, you are fully present. You aren't obsessing about the past or fretting about the future. You are just in the moment, processing events as they happen.[80] When we are mindful, we're more likely to feel calm and safe.

WHY IS MINDFULNESS A GOOD THING?

Compare mindfulness with its opposite, mindlessness. If you lead a busy life, as most of us do, you probably go through your days on autopilot.

Have you ever driven to work and realized you have practically no memories of your trip? Or perhaps you've sat down to eat a meal and read the paper, and suddenly discovered that all the food on your plate has mysteriously vanished? Living mindlessly means missing out on your life. Mindfulness helps you re-engage with the world, moment by moment.

UNDERSTANDING THE DIFFERENCES BETWEEN CLASSIC CBT & MBCT

You can use CBT and MBCT exercises, mixing and matching as you like. However, you need to be aware that they are based on different approaches to mental health. Some people find it easier to stick to one paradigm, and that's fine!

Here are some key points you need to know:

1. **CBT invites you to challenge your thoughts, whereas MBCT encourages you to accept them.**

    Throughout this book, you've been weighing evidence for and against your thoughts. You've been identifying your cognitive distortions, asking other people to share their experiences, and generally gathering a lot of information. Research shows that these techniques work well in people with mild to moderate mental health problems.

    MBCT takes a different approach. Like CBT, it involves noticing destructive thoughts. However, MBCT practitioners teach their clients how to accept them.[81] MBCT techniques help you stay grounded in the present moment and wait for the thoughts to pass, instead of fighting them. You don't actively reframe your approach to the world as you would in CBT.

CBT works because it teaches you how to process your thoughts in a new way and arrive at different conclusions. MBCT works because it teaches you how to move through the world mindfully, accepting and letting go of whatever thoughts come to mind. In simple terms, CBT is analytical and MBCT is more immediate, with a bodily focus—meditation and breathing exercises both involve your senses.

2. **MBCT focuses on preventing depression and anxiety, whereas CBT is used as treatment for people who are already experiencing an episode.**

   MBCT is recommended for people who have experienced multiple episodes of depression.[82] MBCT is also used to help people living with chronic pain or another physical condition.

3. **MBCT does not focus on problem-solving or behavioral activation.**

   Problem-solving is a key skill in CBT because it gives you a framework for taking action. Behavioral activation serves the same purpose; it helps you start taking steps toward changing your environment. MBCT doesn't emphasize these techniques. MBCT is about "being," whereas CBT is about "doing."

4. **MBCT is usually delivered in group therapy format.**
   MBCT is normally given in a structured group format that lasts several weeks. Clients are asked to practice new techniques they have learned between sessions. During

their classes, they have the opportunity to practice together and receive guidance from an MBCT-trained therapist.

However, this doesn't mean you can't benefit from some of the techniques used in MBCT. Some research suggests that group and individual therapy are equally effective.[83]

Here are three exercises you can try. They are similar to those practiced in MBCT classes.

MBCT Exercise #1: Body Scanning

Sit or lie down somewhere that is comfortable. Some people find this exercise so relaxing that they fall asleep, so if it isn't bedtime, do your body scan in a chair rather than on your bed.

Start by bringing your awareness to your entire body. Notice the weight of your body against the chair or the bed. Inhale, hold the air in your lungs for a few seconds, then exhale. Repeat this several times.

Next, focus on your feet. Notice their weight and temperature. Move your awareness up to your lower legs, then your thighs, buttocks, and trunk. Pay attention to how your back feels against the bed or chair.

Pay attention to your shoulders. If they are hunched or tight, take a deep breath and let them drop. Is your jaw clenched? Let it soften. If your hands are balled into fists, exhale and deliberately relax your fingers.

Repeat this exercise at least three times per day, for 20 minutes each time.

MBCT Exercise #2: Mindful Eating

For this exercise, you will need a small piece of food that you can chew or suck for a few minutes. A raisin or a piece of hard candy is perfect.

Find a place that's quiet where you won't be interrupted for five minutes. Hold the food in one hand. Notice how it feels against your skin. What temperature is it? How would you describe its texture? Put it up to the light. What color is it?

Now, smell the food. How would you describe it? Does it have a strong or subtle smell? Is it appetizing? When you really pay attention to your usual snacks, you might be surprised to find that you don't enjoy them quite as much as you think!

Next, put the food in your mouth. Don't bite into it yet. Roll the food on your tongue. What does it taste like? Is it sharp, sweet, salty, bitter, or a combination? What is the texture like? Is it dry, moist, or somewhere in between?

Finally, swallow the food. Feel it go down your throat and into your stomach. Was it easy to swallow?

This is a great exercise to do at the start of a meal. You will automatically eat more slowly, which will help you digest your food. It's also useful if you have a problem with overeating or binging; checking in at the start of a meal or snack helps you pay attention to your body's cues. It's not a magic cure, but it can encourage you to stop eating when you start to feel full.

MBCT Exercise #3: Walking Meditation

Most people assume that you need to sit still for hours in the lotus position to meditate. Fortunately for those of us who find it hard to sit in silence for longer than a couple of minutes, this isn't the case! You can try a walking meditation instead.

If possible, choose surroundings that are green and calm. Relax your shoulders and maintain a good posture. As you step forward, notice how it feels when your foot meets the ground. What does the earth or tarmac feel like beneath your feet?

As you walk, use all your senses. What can you hear? What can you smell? What can you see? Look up—are there any interesting clouds in the sky? Take a few deep breaths. What does the air feel like in your lungs?

If it's raining, you can do this exercise indoors if you have a large room or clear hallway.

WHAT TO DO IF YOUR MIND JUST WON'T STAY STILL

Mindfulness and meditation practices are simple, but that doesn't mean they are easy. The biggest obstacle will be your mental chatter. When you slow down and let yourself notice your thoughts, you'll notice just how noisy your brain is. It's normal for your mind to leap from thought to thought, worry to worry, or idea to idea. The Buddhists have a term for this phenomenon. They call it the "monkey mind," because the mind is rather like a monkey, swinging quickly from branch to branch.[84]

No one, however long they have been practicing mindfulness exercises, has a completely still mind. The difference between novice and expert practitioners is that the latter have long ago accepted that their brains will always be hyperactive. However, they aren't bothered. They know that being mindful isn't about removing every thought from your brain. Neither is it about becoming a cold, stoic robot.

RADICAL ACCEPTANCE

Radical acceptance is a technique developed by psychologist Marsha Linehan. In the 1980s, Linehan devised a form of therapy called Dialectical Behavior Therapy, or DBT. As you learned in Chapter 1, DBT is a treatment that helps clients understand how their thoughts and behaviors work together, and why personal change involves both accepting yourself and your thoughts and behaviors as they are and setting goals for the future.

Lots of people struggle to confront reality, but this is the first step to change. To help her clients make peace with difficult situations, Linehan suggested they try radical acceptance.[85]

Exercise: Radical Acceptance

You can either wait until you are in a difficult situation to try this technique, or you can practice it by deliberately thinking about something that makes you angry or upset.

Start by telling yourself that you don't have to approve of a situation to accept it. Take a few deep breaths. Say to yourself, "OK, this is happening. I don't have to do anything about it. I don't have to fight it. I just have to let it be, and it will pass."

This exercise is harder than it sounds! Your mind will still spin, and you'll still feel the urge to blame someone or something for your misfortune. When this happens, bring your attention back to your breathing.

When you feel a little calmer, ask yourself these questions:

1. What led up to this event?
2. Did you play a part in causing this problem?
3. What part did other people play?
4. Did luck come into it?
5. You have a choice—you can choose to accept the situation or rail against it. Which approach do you think will be more constructive?

We like to think that, with enough effort, we can control everything in our lives. It's a comforting illusion. However, it just isn't true. Life is unfair sometimes, and it's often unpredictable. Learning to accept life as it is may be scary, but it is enormously liberating.

SUMMARY

- CBT therapists are increasingly using mindfulness in their work with clients.
- Mindfulness exercises ground you in the present moment, freeing you from worries about the past or the future.
- Mindfulness Based Cognitive Therapy (MBCT) is a structured form of therapy that draws on principles of both CBT and mindfulness.
- You can use some MBCT-style techniques for yourself, such as mindful eating and meditation.
- Mindful acceptance or "radical acceptance" can help you make peace with whatever life throws your way.

CONCLUSION

You should feel very proud of yourself. You've taken a long, hard look at your destructive thought patterns, and you've started to think and behave in brand new ways. That takes courage and determination. Your efforts will soon pay off—assuming they haven't already made a difference. People and situations that used to drag you down won't seem like such a big deal. Sure, you'll still face the normal trials of everyday life, but you'll be better at shaking them off.

CBT techniques get easier the more you practice them. It's like driving a car. It feels awkward and complicated at first, but it becomes second nature within a few months. Spending time and money on driving lessons is well worth the effort because then you get to drive for the rest of your life. The same goes for CBT. Train your brain now, and you'll reap the benefits for decades.

Until recently, therapy was taboo. Thankfully, more people are realizing that therapy isn't just for people with diagnosed mental health problems and we can all benefit from learning how to stop negative thoughts from taking over our lives. So, when your family and friends ask why you are so much happier, why not be honest and tell them about how CBT has changed your life?

You could tell them to read this book, or even tell them exactly how you use cognitive restructuring, exposure therapy or other CBT techniques. The more people learn about how the human mind works, the healthier our society will become.

Just imagine how many people would benefit from learning basic CBT principles. You can play your part in starting a CBT revolution.

If you take only one thing away from this book, let it be this: You aren't at the mercy of your thoughts or emotions. They might feel overwhelming, but don't be fooled. Ultimately, you are the one in control. Realizing this simple but powerful truth is the first step toward real empowerment.

THANKS FOR READING!

I really hope you enjoyed this book and, most of all, got more value from it than you had to give.

It would mean a lot to me if you left an Amazon review—I will reply to all questions asked!

Simply find this book on Amazon, scroll to the reviews section, and click "Write a customer review".

Or alternatively please visit www.pristinepublish.com/cbtbundlereview to leave a review.

Be sure to check out my email list, where I am constantly adding tons of value. The best way to get on the list currently is by visiting www.pristinepublish.com/meditationbonus and entering your email.

Here I'll provide actionable information that aims to improve your enjoyment of life. I'll update you on my latest books, and I'll even send free e-books that I think you'll find useful.

Kindest regards,

Olivia Telford

Also by
Olivia Telford

With Hygge and Minimalism you'll discover something that offers relaxation, happiness, and contentment, all rolled into one. They encompass the positivity and enjoyment that one can get from simple everyday things.

Visit: www.pristinepublish.com/olivia

MINDFULNESS

The Remarkable Truth
Behind Meditation and Being
Present in Your Life

OLIVIA TELFORD

CONTENTS

INTRODUCTION

Imagine a treatment for anxiety, everyday stress, and depression that:

- Doesn't involve drugs
- Has no unpleasant side-effects
- Costs nothing
- Is available anywhere
- Can be used by anyone
- Has been scientifically proven to work

There really is a solution that ticks all these boxes. It's called "mindfulness." In this book, you're going to learn what mindfulness is, how to make it part of your everyday routine, and how it can transform your life.

You'll discover simple practices to help you feel better on every level – physically, psychologically, and spiritually. By the end of the book, you'll see the world, and yourself, in a whole new way. The future will feel less scary. The past will no longer cause you pain. You'll find it easier to forgive yourself and others, develop self-compassion, and find inner peace.

The only tools you need are an open mind and patience. You don't need to invest in special equipment, go on any retreats, or change your religious beliefs. You definitely don't need to become a Buddhist monk, renounce the modern world, or live a minimalist life.

At the same time, this book will challenge you to examine your values and lifestyle. For example, you'll be encouraged to ask yourself some tough questions about how you spend your time. The path ahead will be challenging, but it could be the most important journey of your life.

Perhaps you've tried therapy, self-help books, medication, and support groups. Maybe these measures helped for a while, but they didn't lead to real change. It's time to try a new approach.

Mindfulness is a way of life. It lets you befriend your authentic self, the real "you" hiding under years of social conditioning and unhealthy habits. When you accept yourself, you can take your life in a new direction. This sounds like a paradox, but by the time you finish this book, this simple idea will make perfect sense.

Are you ready? Turn the page to begin.

WHAT OTHERS ARE SAYING ABOUT MINDFULNESS

"Looking to rid stress and live more freely? In Mindfulness by Olivia Telford you will find comprehensive and straightforward techniques you can use today to instantly improve your well-being. After reading this book, I've never felt more empowered, happier and productive. Whether you've tried meditation before or are brand new to it, this is the perfect guide."

—*Judy Dyer, author of* Empath: A Complete Guide for Developing Your Gift and Finding Your Sense of Self

"An amazing little guide to the good life! Olivia Telford explains what mindfulness is, why it's so important, and how to cultivate it. Simple, actionable, and deeply insightful. I highly recommend this book!"

—Patrik Edblad, author of The Self-Discipline Blueprint: A Simple Guide to Beat Procrastination, Achieve Your Goals, and Get the Life You Want

"It's one thing to meditate, but it's a whole other thing to embody Presence throughout one's everyday life. While meditation can bring tremendous benefits, the real life-changing results come when you can infuse Presence into all aspects of your inner and outer life so that you live with true mindfulness. Olivia

Telford has done the world a great service by writing a book that is packed with authentic exercises that allow you to become more mindful and present in many different aspects of your life. Whether you're new to meditative and mindfulness practices or have been practicing for years, this book can serve you in profound ways."

—Ziad Masri, author of Reality Unveiled: The Hidden Keys of Existence That Will Transform Your Life (and the World)

"A powerful, enlightening book that works its way into your heart and soul."

—Bella Jean, author of The Forever In Between: A Historical Western Romance Book

"A stellar job by Olivia Telford. Another one, really. I was never quite a 100% believer in the concept of mindfulness, but I get it now. I really do. For me, the best part really starts from Telford's telling of Buddhism and how that kickstarts and underlies the whole process. When you look at it that way, and through the lens of detachment from everything, then you can really start to make headway. It's a great read."

—Peter Hollins, author of The Science of Self-Learning: How to Teach Yourself Anything, Learn More in Less Time, and Direct Your Own Education

JOIN OUR MINDFULNESS GROUP

In order to maximize the value you receive from this book, I highly encourage you to join our tight-knit community on Facebook. Here you will be able to connect and share strategies with others practicing mindfulness and meditation in order to continue your growth.

Taking this journey alone is not recommended, and this can be an excellent support network for you.

It would be great to connect with you there,

Olivia Telford

To Join, Visit:
www.pristinepublish.com/mindfulgroup

CHAPTER 1:

WHAT IS MINDFULNESS?

"Mindfulness" has become a buzzword in personal development circles. You may have seen articles, magazines, and websites about it. Maybe you've seen ads for mindfulness classes, or you might have been offered mindfulness seminars at work.

MINDFULNESS IN A SINGLE SENTENCE

According to Mindful magazine, mindfulness can be summed up as:

> "...the basic human ability to be fully present, aware of where we are and what we're doing, and not overly reactive or overwhelmed by what's going on around us."[86]

Psychologist Shauna Shapiro, an internationally renowned mindfulness expert, explains that there are three key components to mindfulness:[87]

1. Intention, or "paying attention on purpose"
2. Attention
3. Attitude, specifically an attitude of non-judgmental acceptance

At first glance, the whole topic of mindfulness seems odd or re-dundant. After all, aren't we all aware of what we're doing?

Unfortunately, the answer is "No." Most of us go through life on autopilot. Our thoughts and emotions control us, not the other way around. Anxiety, stress, and depression are endemic in modern society. Too many of us feel out of control, scared, and overwhelmed. Mindfulness is about learning how to accept and work with your mind – and yourself. By extension, it's also about accepting your life and discovering the joy in ordinary, everyday moments.

MINDFULNESS VERSUS MINDLESSNESS

You can think of mindfulness as the opposite of mindless action. When we behave mindlessly, we zone out. We stop experiencing our own lives. For example, have you ever sat down to eat a meal, only to get distracted by your phone, your own racing thoughts, or the view from your window?

If so, did you look down at your plate and realize that all the food was gone? Lots of us do this. Just think of how many meals the average person eats without even tasting them! Mindless eating isn't satisfying, and it can even make you gain weight. Later in the book, you'll learn how to gain control over mindless behaviors and unhelpful habits.

Mindfulness Exercise: An Introduction To Mindfulness

To appreciate what mindfulness means, you need to experience it for yourself. Try this exercise to help you gain insight into how it feels to live mindfully.

Step 1: Go outside and find a leaf. If you can't find one, a small pebble will also work.

Step 2: Set a timer for five minutes.

Step 3: Look at the leaf as though you've never seen a leaf before. Turn it over slowly. Take in its color, shape, weight, and texture. Put it up to the light. How does the color change? If your mind starts to wander, bring your attention back to the leaf.

This simple practice shows you what mindfulness is all about. By focusing all your attention on a single object, you have no choice but to live in the present.

Mindfulness Exercise: Tracking Your Wandering Mind

Keep a pen and paper with you throughout the day. Every time you catch your mind wandering away from your current task, make a mark on the piece of paper. It should only take you a few hours to see why mindfulness will benefit you.

WHERE DID MINDFULNESS COME FROM?

Modern mindfulness practices have ancient roots. In Buddhism, it's at the heart of spiritual practice. To understand the link between Buddhism and mindfulness today, it's helpful to understand what Buddhism teaches about the mind.

The Buddha taught his followers that most human suffering is self-generated. Although external events can cause us pain, it's how we think about and respond to these events that matters most.

He also believed that humans make themselves unhappy by grasping after things they don't already have, such as relationships and material possessions. As long as we have these "cravings," we will never be satisfied. The key to inner peace is to understand, and then detach ourselves from, these cravings.

Common cravings include the desire for money, status, and beauty. There is nothing intrinsically wrong with wanting these things, but when we start making them the central focus of our lives, we're in trouble. For example, aiming for a promotion is all well and good, but working so hard that you lose sight of your values and alienate your family is not.

So, how can we learn to identify and overcome these cravings? Buddhists turn to meditation, among other methods, to help them become aware of their cravings. Gaining insight into the workings of one's own mind is a key step to overcoming suffering.

THE DIFFERENCE BETWEEN MINDFULNESS & MEDITATION

"Mindfulness" and "meditation" are often used interchangeably, but it's important to be clear on the differences.

Meditation is normally a formal, seated practice. There are several types, including mantra-based meditation, guided meditation, and loving-kindness meditation. We'll take a closer look at these practices in later chapters.

You have to make time for a meditation session. Meditators usually start a session with a goal in mind, such as sending love to someone else. They normally begin with breathing exercises that allow them to focus on inhalation and exhalation. The meditator then "turns inward," focusing on an idea, word, or an external object such as a candle flame.

Mindfulness can take the form of meditation, but it goes beyond formal practice. You can be mindful anywhere. There's no need to sit down and contemplate a single idea or object. In summary, you don't have to practice meditation to be mindful. However, formal meditation is well worth a go, because scientific research has demonstrated the positive effects it has on the mind and body.

Mindfulness doesn't solve your problems. Instead, it provides you with a space to simply sit with them, and accept your situation for what it is. Buddhists refer to mindfulness practices as sati.[88] In this book, you'll learn how to integrate mindfulness into your everyday life.

THE SATIPATTHANA SUTTA

Known as the "Discourse on the Foundations of Mindfulness," the Satipatthana Sutta is generally considered the most important Buddhist text on mindfulness meditation. The text outlines Buddha's teachings on mindfulness, framing it as an essential faculty anyone can develop.

According to the Sutta, mindfulness has to be deliberately cultivated. Buddha acknowledged that practicing it isn't easy. Satipatthana meditation encourages personal insight but also improves general concentration. In this context, "insight" means a keen awareness of seeing reality, perhaps for the first time.[89]

The Buddha frequently referred to the Four Foundations of Mindfulness:[90]

1. Body: When you are mindful, you notice how it feels to live in your body. You notice your breathing patterns, posture, and any aches, pains, or itching. The Buddha taught his followers to think of their bodies, not as a possession, but merely a home or vehicle they happen to be inhabiting. Breathing exercises are an effective means of getting in touch with the body. We'll come back to the breath many times in this book.

2. Feelings: Mindful people are willing to face their feelings, knowing that all emotions are transient. They are prepared to label feelings as they arise, watching them come and go. Mindfulness teaches us that our feelings don't have to define us as individuals.

3. Consciousness: Mindful people acknowledge not only their emotions but their general state of mind. For instance, during a mindfulness session, you may acknowledge that you are "tired" or "content."

4. Dharma: This Sanskrit word is hard to define in English. Roughly translated, it means "the nature of things" or "law of nature." It can refer to Buddhist teaching, but it can also be used to describe the world around us. Everyone carries their own history and set of experiences, so Buddhists say that everyone's dharma is different. Someone in tune with their personal dharma is following their unique path, or calling.

This book isn't an in-depth discussion of Buddhist philosophy, but it's helpful to understand the roots of contemporary mindfulness. If you'd like to learn more about Buddhist teachings, The Buddhist Society (thebuddhistsociety.org) is a good place to start.

How Buddhist Ideas Entered Western Medicine

In the 1970s, biologist Professor Jon Kabat-Zinn pioneered a new approach for people living with chronic illness. Over an eight-week period, he trialed a stress-reduction program based on mindfulness practices. The course, which is offered at the Center for Mindfulness at UMASS Medical School, teaches people how to use mindful activity to cope with day-to-day stress and chronic pain.[91]

Although he was heavily influenced by Buddhist teachings as a student, Kabat-Zinn teaches mindfulness from a secular perspective. Mindfulness researchers aren't usually very interested in learning complex Buddhist philosophy. Instead, they concentrate on teaching and implementing exercises that improve a person's mental and physical health.

Kabat-Zinn's approach is now known as Mindfulness-Based Stress Reduction, or MBSR. We'll take a closer look at the principles underlying MBSR later in the book. Since those early days, mindfulness has become a popular tool for therapists, trainers, educators, and coaches. Hundreds of peer-reviewed studies have shown it to be effective for people with anxiety, depression, stress, eating disorders, and other forms of emotional distress. MBSR is still taught today, at dozens of centers across the US.

Why Do We Need Mindfulness?

In the Western world, stress and mental illness are at an all-time high. One possible cause is our hectic lifestyles. Most of us have to balance a job and a family, and we are working long hours just to make ends meet. There are also many global problems to worry about. Thanks to the internet, it's easier than ever to read about the financial insecurity, climate change, and political turmoil that threaten us.

We also have to contend with social media. Scrolling through profiles and feeds that show other people enjoying themselves can be disheartening, and encourage us to make unhelpful comparisons. If we don't measure up to our peers, or to society's standards, we feel inferior and depressed.

In summary, we have plenty to worry about in the 21st century. We need psychological defenses against the stressors in our lives.

If we are to solve society's problems, we need to work together. For that to happen, we need to value others and take the time to see their point of view. Mindfulness can help us adopt a compassionate attitude and increase our empathy.

For example, a study published in Psychological Science showed that people who went on an eight-week meditation course were three times more likely to help out a stranger in need than those in the control condition.[92] If enough of us learn to be mindful of others and tune into their suffering, society could change in a profound way.

WHAT DOES THE RESEARCH SAY?

Mindfulness isn't just appealing on a common-sense level. It's also backed up by rigorous scientific research.

Here are a few key findings from the last two decades of research:

1. **Mindfulness makes you more resilient in the face of stress**

   Mindfulness practices can't make life's problems disappear. However, they can help stabilize you during life's more trying moments. Research with students shows that learning and practicing mindfulness skills significantly lowers stress and risk of burnout.[93]

2. **Mindfulness can improve your relationships**

   Married couples who score higher on measures of mindfulness are happier.[94] This makes sense; if you are mindful in your relationships, you'll be better at staying calm when things get tough. You'll also be better at understanding and communicating your own emotions without resorting to angry or impatient outbursts. In the long run, this could have huge implications. How many divorces could be prevented if couples learned how to approach their differences in a mindful way?

3. **Mindfulness can enhance your working memory**
   One of the most exciting benefits of mindfulness is the effect it has on cognitive functioning. The term "cognitive functioning" refers to the day-to-day mental tasks we all have to do. Someone with good cognitive functioning can plan tasks, stay focused, and commit new information to memory.

   In one study, participants were split into two groups. One group was given four meditation training sessions, and the other was invited to listen to an audiobook instead. The people in the meditation session enjoyed a significant drop in fatigue and anxiety and achieved higher scores on memory tests.[95]

   If you often forget things, you might assume you are just cursed with a poor memory. However, mindlessness is more likely to be the real cause of your woes. To remember something, you need to take in new information. Otherwise, you won't be able to recall it later. By learning how to be mindful of your surroundings, you'll feel less flustered and forgetful.

4. **Mindfulness can improve your physical health**
   Although more research is needed, there's plenty of evidence to suggest that mindfulness can improve your physical health. For example, psychologists have discov-

ered that mindfulness can strengthen your immune system and reduce chronic inflammation. It's still early, but some researchers have speculated that regular mindfulness practices could even slow down the aging process.[96]

5. **Mindfulness can help you make better choices**
Our lives are defined by our decisions. Unfortunately, it's all too easy to make hasty choices that don't benefit us or other people. Mindfulness practices teach you how to make sound decisions based on the facts in front of you, rather than your emotions or irrational fears.

Note that being mindful isn't about pushing your emotions to one side and acting like a robot. It's about understanding how to tame them when they work against you. Staying mindful lets you avoid making poor decisions that come back to haunt you later.

You've Nothing To Lose & Everything To Gain

In summary, mindfulness offers a lot of benefits – all for a minimal time investment. No matter how busy you are, mindfulness can become part of your daily routine. Most of the exercises in this book take 10 minutes or less. You can extend your sessions if you like, but you only need a short period of time to feel the difference.

Summary

- Mindfulness is the act of paying attention.
- Mindfulness is not the same thing as meditation. Although meditation is a useful way to practice mindfulness, it is only one path.

- Mindfulness is rooted in Buddhism, but you don't need to change your religious beliefs to use mindfulness.
- Mindfulness offers lots of physical and psychological benefits, including reduced stress and a more effective immune system.

CHAPTER 2:

SIMPLE MINDFULNESS EXERCISES

I n the last chapter, you got a brief taste of mindfulness. In this chapter, you'll learn several more exercises that will help you lead a more mindful life.

Later in this book, you'll discover how mindfulness can help you overcome specific problems, such as depression and anxiety. We'll also talk about how it can be used as an anti-procrastination and goal-setting tool.

First, we're going to cover three practices that take less than five minutes. These are general exercises that you can use any time. Think of them as multipurpose tools; whatever your specific problem or situation, they will equip you with the basic skills you need to start your journey to mindfulness.

The more you use these tools, the better. Try each one several times. If you like it, continue; if not, experiment with another.

THREE SIMPLE MINDFULNESS PRACTICES

Simple Mindfulness Practice #1: Mindful Breathing

Watching your breath is the simplest practice of all. The aim is to breathe as usual while attending to the sensations in your body.

1. Sit or lie down. If you are feeling tired, it may be best to sit up so you don't fall asleep.
2. Close your eyes if you prefer.
3. Pay attention to your breathing. Observe how it feels to inhale and exhale air.
4. If your thoughts start wandering off, bring your focus back to your breath.

SIMPLE MINDFULNESS PRACTICE #2: TASTING FOOD

We take the act of eating for granted, but when was the last time you slowed down and really appreciated a meal or snack? This practice uses food as a focal point of awareness.

Follow these steps:[97]

1. Choose a small piece of food, such as a raisin or a nut.
2. Look at the food carefully. Notice what it looks like, how it feels in your hands, and how it smells.
3. Put the food in your mouth. Notice how it tastes. Move it around your mouth for a couple of minutes. Finally, chew it carefully and swallow.
4. Pay attention to the sensation of the food moving down your throat and into your stomach.

You'll probably notice various thoughts popping into your head. For example, you might think, "I don't like raisins" or "This is dumb, what's the point?"

That's OK. You don't have to empty your head of all thoughts. Your mission is to keep your attention on the present moment as much as possible. If your mind wanders off, just bring it back to the task at hand.

SIMPLE MINDFULNESS PRACTICE #3: LISTENING TO MUSIC

Any kind of music can be a meditation tool, but choosing a soothing track will make the experience more relaxing.

1. Sit or lie down in a comfortable position.
2. Play the music.
3. Follow each note. Pay attention to the pitch and tempo. If your mind conjures up images or memories, observe them. Don't wish them away. Just notice how your brain and body respond to the sounds.
4. As the track comes to an end, pay attention to how your body feels. Does it feel lighter? Softer? Heavier? Just notice.
5. Pay attention to your mood. Do you feel calmer? Un-moved? Uncomfortable? Whatever you feel is perfectly normal. There is no "correct" response here. The aim is to practice noticing what is going on in your mind and body.

If you use public transport, why not try this exercise on your journey to work? It will put you in a calm frame of mind that will help you face the day ahead. You can also use it on the way home to decompress after a stressful day in the office.

LONGER PRACTICES

If you have more than five minutes to spare, try a body scan or a mindful walk. Once or twice a week is enough, especially when you're first starting out. Take it easy. Do what fits into your lifestyle.

Mindfulness Exercise: Body Scanning

Body scanning makes for a wonderfully relaxing start or end to your day:[98]

1. Set aside at least half an hour, but an hour is best. Give yourself the chance to feel the benefits of this exercise.
2. Lie down on a comfortable surface. You may wish to place a small cushion or folded blanket beneath your head. Turn off any bright lights.
3. Close your eyes.
4. Notice your breath. Notice how it feels to breathe in and out. If your mind drifts away, bring your attention back to the flow of air in and out of your body.
5. Inhale and switch your attention to any part of your body. Follow your intuition.
6. Notice any sensations that arise. You may notice tingling, warmth, numbness, aching, lightness, fullness – or a combination of the above. Some people prefer to begin at the head and move downward, while others start with their feet. Take an attitude of curiosity rather than judgment.
7. When you have finished scanning your body, focus on your breathing again. When you're ready, open your eyes and sit up.

Mindfulness Exercise: Mindful Walking

Research has shown that walking in a green space, such as a park, improves your mood and sharpens your concentration. You'll also benefit from moving your body because exercise helps you sleep better. If you spend a lot of time sitting down during the day, walking may be more appealing than seated practices.

Here's how to take a mindful walk:[99]

1. Before you begin walking, tune into your body. Notice your posture and temperature. Feel the sensation of your feet on the ground. How do they feel inside your shoes?
2. Start walking. Move slightly slower than usual.
3. As you walk, notice how your heels, then your toes make contact with the ground.
4. Take deep breaths, noticing how it feels to breathe in and out.
5. Keep your gaze soft.
6. When emotions and thoughts pop up, acknowledge them without judgment or condemnation.
7. Walk in this way for as long as you like.
8. End your practice slowly. Give yourself a few seconds to feel the earth beneath your feet.

Any of the exercises in this chapter will help you feel less stressed. They are all perfect for taking a bit of time out of a busy day.

SUMMARY

- The three simplest mindfulness exercises involve focusing on your breath, tasting some food, and listening to a piece of music.
- Body scanning is a longer practice but is well worth trying if you have the time.
- Mindful walking is a great alternative if you feel too restless to sit still or lie down.
- You don't have to use all the practices in this chapter. Using one or two a few times per week is enough to trigger real change.

CHAPTER 3:

HOW TO MEDITATE

You don't have to start meditating to lead a mindful life, but give it a try — you'll be glad you did! Meditation reduces stress, helps reduce anxiety, enhances your attention span, improves your memory, lowers your blood pressure, and promotes better sleep.[100]

In this chapter, you'll experiment with three types of meditation. We're going to look at mantra meditation, loving-kindness meditation, and guided meditation.

MEDITATING FOR THE FIRST TIME

Keep your expectations realistic, otherwise you may become discouraged and give up. Not many people can sit down and meditate for an hour on their first attempt. (Not that you need to meditate for this long anyway!) It takes time to cultivate your attention span, so aim to meditate for five minutes at first. Twenty or thirty minutes per day is ideal, but a few times per week is much better than nothing.

Be prepared to experience a range of emotions. You may feel self-conscious, anxious, or frustrated. This is completely normal! Sit with these feelings. Notice them come and go. Gently bring your attention back to your breath, mantra, or other primary focus of your practice.

MANTRA MEDITATION

"Mantra" is a Sanskrit term derived from two roots, "man" and "trai." "Man" translates as "to think" or "mind," and "trai" means "tool," "protect," or "free from." Therefore, a mantra is a tool used to liberate the mind.[101]

Mantra meditation involves focusing on, and repeating, a mantra. Mantras are not usually spoken aloud but repeated internally by your inner voice. A mantra provides a point of fixation for your mind during meditation. It's hard to focus on two or more thoughts at once. By using a mantra, you cut through mental chatter and stay in the present moment.

Here's how to get started:[102]

1. Pick a mantra. Mantras should be short, positive, and easy to repeat. Some people prefer traditional mantras such as "Om" or "Sat, Chit, Ananda." Using a mantra in a language you don't understand can help you concentrate, because it is less likely to trigger your emotions than English words or phrases.

    However, you may find that an English mantra holds more appeal. Experiment with both to find what works for you. Popular mantras include "I am enough," "I change my thoughts, I change my world," and "I love you, I am sorry, please forgive me, thank you."

2. Sit down in a quiet place, free from distractions.

3. Close your eyes. You can meditate with your eyes open, but most people find that closing their eyes helps them focus their attention.

4. Set your intention. Decide why you are meditating right here, right now. For example, do you want to calm yourself down? Or perhaps you want to feel a sense of kinship with those around you?

5. Ground yourself with some deep breathing. Spend a couple of minutes watching your breath. Inhale and exhale, feeling air fill and leave your lungs.

6. Begin repeating your mantra. Keep a steady rhythm. If it feels right, you can chant it aloud.

7. When your mind wanders, pull your focus back to the mantra. At first, you'll have to do this every few seconds.

8. Repeat your mantra for as long as you like.

Loving-Kindness Meditation

Loving-kindness meditation, also known as "metta meditation," helps you foster goodwill towards yourself and others.

Here's how to do it:[103]

1. With your eyes closed, sit in a comfortable position.

2. Take a few deep breaths.

3. Begin by receiving love from others. Imagine that someone who has shown you kindness, such as a family member or teacher, is standing to your right. Feel the love emanating from them. Now, imagine another person you love and admire standing to your left. Again, feel their love and compassion. Alternatively, you can imagine that the same person is standing on both your left and right sides.

4. Now picture yourself surrounded by everyone who cares for you. Welcome their love and care. Let yourself feel warm, safe, and protected.

5. Think about the person standing to your right. Send them love. Say to them, "May you live with ease, may you be happy, may you be free from pain."

6. Repeat #5, but this time, direct your love to the person on your left.

7. Next, think of a neutral person in your life. This should be someone you neither like nor dislike, such as the person who sometimes serves you at the grocery store. Say to them, "Just as I wish to, may you also live with ease and happiness."

8. Repeat #7, but this time, send your good wishes out to the world as a whole. It may help to picture the earth as a globe. You could picture it from space, or as a small ball directly in front of you.

Some people also send love and warm wishes to people they actively dislike. This can be healing, but may also stir up some difficult emotions. Start with the practice above, and then extend it to those who have harmed you if it feels safe to do so.

GUIDED MEDITATION

As the name implies, guided meditation involves following instructions from someone else. By following their voice, you enter a state of consciousness that helps you relax, accept your negative thoughts, and cope with challenging emotions.

Some guided meditations ask you to focus on your breathing or a mantra. Others are more elaborate, involving lengthy visualizations. For example, your guide may help you enter a mental "safe space" that feels peaceful and serene.

If you want to try guided meditation, you have several options. You can attend a class run by a meditation teacher, or you can buy recordings or CDs you can listen to in the privacy of your own home. There are plenty of free guided meditations online. Here are two sites to get you started:

- https://www.tarabrach.com/guided-meditations/
- https://chopra.com/articles/guided-meditations

You can also write your own guided meditation scripts, record them, and then play them back as you meditate. Hearing your own voice can be strange at first, but after a few sessions, it will feel natural to listen to yourself. Follow a few pre-recorded guided meditations first for inspiration.

RESPECT YOUR MEDITATION TIME

Create a peaceful meditation area in your home. A spare room is ideal, but a corner of your bedroom or living room will work just as well. Make it special. You could buy a new cushion, place some candles in your space, or hang a quote or picture that inspires you. When the weather permits, pick a quiet corner in your garden.

If you live with other people, you may need to get up slightly earlier or go to bed later than usual to carve out some time for yourself, especially if you are a parent. At first, you might feel more tired during the day. Stick with it! Research shows that meditation actually raises your energy levels, meaning you won't miss those 30 minutes of sleep.[104]

SUMMARY

- You don't have to learn to meditate to lead a mindful life, but lots of people find it helpful.
- Mantra meditation involves focusing on a word or phrase.
- Loving-kindness meditation is a wonderful, healing way to send love and warmth to yourself and others. It can help you release grudges or attachments to the past.
- Guided meditations are useful if you want some support. You can attend a class, download meditations, or create your own.

CHAPTER 4:

REDUCING STRESS & NEGATIVITY WITH MINDFULNESS

We all have to deal with stress. Even if you aren't in a high-powered job, live alone, and have few obligations, you still come up against situations that make you feel overwhelmed. In this chapter, we'll look at how mindfulness can reduce your stress levels and help you become a more positive person.

First, a note of caution. You can't lead a stress-free life. Stress is part of the human experience. It's the price we pay for setting goals, living in the real world, and setting high standards for ourselves. A modest amount of stress is actually good for you. For instance, stress can give you the edge at work, giving you the buzz you need to get a project done.

WHEN STRESS BECOMES HARMFUL

Although some stress is beneficial, prolonged stress has a devastating effect on our minds and bodies. When you feel stressed, your body releases a hormone called cortisol. Cortisol is useful during emergency situations because it raises our blood sugar and gives our muscles easier access to energy reserves.

However, research has shown a link between elevated cortisol and serious diseases such as type 2 diabetes. Scientists have also discovered that heightened cortisol levels may be associated with obesity. Cortisol can encourage your body to store excess fat around your abdomen. This pattern of fat distribution increases your risk of diabetes and heart disease.[105]

So, can mindfulness help get your cortisol levels under control? Absolutely! A study published in the journal *Neuropsychobiology* showed that cortisol levels drop significantly after just 8 weeks of mindfulness training. The researchers also measured cortisol levels in long-term meditators and found that the longer they had been practicing meditation, the less cortisol there was in their blood.[106]

MINDFULNESS & LETTING GO

Many of us are addicted to the idea of being in control. We like to think that we can control our relationships, our children, our careers, our finances, and so on. To some extent, this is correct. The way you conduct yourself at work, for example, can make the difference when it comes to getting a promotion.

Unfortunately, the reality is that many events are beyond our control. When something happens that makes us realize this uncomfortable truth, we get upset and stressed. To continue the example above, you can choose how much effort you put into your job, but if the board of directors decides that they need to lay off dozens of people, there's not much you can do about it. In times like these, you need to anticipate, accept, and cope with stress instead of lamenting the unfairness of life.

The prospect of accepting reality for what it is, not what we want it to be, can be terrifying. Buddhists are keenly aware of this. They believe that our addiction to control is an unhealthy attachment that only results in suffering.

Paradoxically, the better you are at accepting your distress and anxiety in any given situation, the happier you will become. When you develop self-compassion and self-acceptance, your stress will pass quicker, leaving you with time and energy to plan your next move.

Mindfulness Isn't The Same As Apathy

You might assume that if you give up fighting for control, you'll give up on life altogether. Society teaches us that those who set inflexible goals and push themselves to succeed are to be praised and admired, so it's hardly surprising that any notion of accepting the natural ups and downs of life seems suspicious.

The key to leading a more relaxed life is to accept that the only thing you can really control in life is your response to it. As you practice mindfulness, you'll come to appreciate that this is an empowering position.

After all, if you can't control the world around you, you are free to focus on how you react. This doesn't mean you can't make plans for your future or set goals, merely that you realize everything is impermanent. Few things work out exactly as we hope.

Noticing Stress In Your Body

Having accepted that stress is normal and inevitable, the next step is to train yourself how to pick up on your early warning signs. Mindfulness is a great stress detector!

Some of us are so out of touch with our own bodies that we don't even realize when they are starting to show the signs of strain.

Here are some clues that your stress levels are rising:

- Your head feels foggy, you're tired, and you find it hard to concentrate.
- Your appetite changes; some people eat more under stress, whereas others can't face food.
- Your muscles feel tense.
- You feel as though you could cry at any moment.
- You have a headache or migraine.
- You experience palpitations.
- You seem to be sweating more than usual.
- Your skin feels itchy; if you suffer from eczema, it may feel more irritated than usual.

Use the basic mindfulness exercises in Chapter Two to check in with yourself throughout the day. You may be surprised to learn that you are considerably more stressed than you imagined. That's normal! The busier and more stressed you are, the less likely you are to slow down for a few minutes and think about what's actually going on in your body.

How To Handle The Signs Of Stress

Often, merely tuning into your body and sitting with your feelings is enough to lower your stress levels. Accepting what is happening around you and within you fosters acceptance, and it gives you the chance to learn that all emotions pass.

The following exercise will help you cope with short-term stress.

Mindfulness Exercise: Riding The Wave Of Stress

The next time you start feeling annoyed or agitated, try this quick exercise that allows you to ride out stress instead of fighting it:[107]

1. Wherever you are, stand or sit still.
2. Take a deep breath, then briefly scan your body from your head to your feet.
3. Watch for signs of stress. Are your hands curling into fists? Are you sweating? Are your shoulders tense?
4. Imagine that your stress is like a large wave, crashing towards you.
5. As the wave reaches its peak, picture yourself literally riding or surfing it. Picture yourself sitting or standing on the peak, confident yet serene.
6. Let yourself feel content and proud for negotiating the wave, whilst remembering that you will need to keep doing this throughout your life.

Mindfulness, Long-Term Stress, & Burnout

So far, we've talked about short-term stress – those everyday moments that make you feel overwhelmed. But what about stress that accumulates over time? The kind of stress that leaves you feeling burned out and depleted?

Burnout can happen to anyone, including stay-at-home parents and students. It's a state of complete physical and emotional exhaustion triggered by a slow build-up of stress, usually over many months. Burnout is a serious health issue, and it can take a long time to recover from the aftereffects.

Here are the most common signs:

- Feeling as though every day is a "bad day."
- No longer finding any sense of purpose or enjoyment in your life or work.
- Feeling taken for granted and underappreciated by everyone around you.
- Feeling tired and drained every day.
- Feeling as though all your tasks are dull, mind-numbing, or repetitive.
- Other physical symptoms include frequent minor illnesses, aches and pains, and changes to your sleep or eating patterns.

Stress is a sign that you care too much about your situation. It's the result of expending too much effort trying to change it. On the other hand, if you are burned out, you start checking out. Nothing seems to matter anymore. You may use drugs, alcohol, or other destructive behaviors to cope. In severe cases, a person with burnout may conclude that life is no longer worth living.

Some people are more prone than others to burnout. Personality is a major factor. If you are a perfectionist with an all-or-nothing thinking style and a love of control, you are at heightened risk. Perfectionists can always find areas for improvement. They find it hard to stop, slow down, and acknowledge their own achievements.

So, how can mindfulness prevent burnout? As you may have guessed, mindfulness helps you let go of things you can't control, which short-circuits stress. Mindfulness also helps you appreciate what is going well, and it gives you breathing space when you find yourself worrying about the future. Finally, living in the present alerts you to the first signs of burnout. The earlier you seek help, the better.

Research shows that mindfulness practice can lower the risk of burnout in high-stress professions. For instance, a review in the *American Journal of Occupational Therapy* concludes that "there is strong evidence for the use of mindfulness practice to reduce job burnout among health care professionals and teachers."[108] If mindfulness works for people in stressful occupations, it probably works for those working in less pressured environments too.

MINDFULNESS & NEGATIVITY

By definition, no one enjoys negative feelings, but they are a fact of life. Even if you have a wonderful job, plenty of money, a loving partner, and lots of friends, there will still be times when life beats you down. Learning to work with your negative emotions will help you weather the storms of life.

Human beings tend to focus on negative, rather than positive events. This is known as the "negativity bias." We all know that it's easier to dwell on the bad things that happen to us during the day, instead of appreciating the highlights.

From an evolutionary perspective, there's a good reason for the negativity bias. Our ancestors needed to remain alert to threats around them. This tendency is great for our survival as a species, but it can make us miserable if we pay too much attention to everything that upsets us.

The human brain is sophisticated, but it reacts to modern inconveniences, such as waiting in a long queue, as though they represent a threat to our lives. In becoming mindful, we learn to accept sadness, fear, and anger so that they no longer have the power to spoil our day.

MINDFULNESS HELPS YOU ACCEPT NEGATIVE EMOTIONS

Most people make the mistake of trying to argue themselves out of their negative emotions. They tell themselves things like:

"Other people have it worse."

"Just pull yourself together."

"Just distract yourself; it's not that hard to forget about it."

Unfortunately, these strategies don't work in the long-term. They might work to temporarily stuff down the pain, but they are all forms of avoidance. Avoiding feelings only creates further tension and fear, which results in more negativity.

As spiritual teacher and writer Eckhart Tolle notes, "What you resist, persists." If you want to recover from your scariest feelings, you must embrace them.

Mindfulness Exercise: Working With Negative Emotions

Mindfulness expert Melli O'Brien, also known as "Mrs. Mindfulness," offers this six-step practice you can use when you feel swamped by negative emotions:[109]

1. As soon as you realize that you're feeling a negative emotion, take a moment to pause. Take a few deep breaths.
2. Let yourself acknowledge that you are experiencing the emotion. Say, "There is [emotion] in me" or "I feel [emotion]."
3. Hold the emotion. Accept that it's there. Don't fight it. Your mind may conjure up a mental image, perhaps of the situation that triggered the emotion. Whatever comes up, sit with it. After a couple of minutes, you'll realize that even the strongest emotion doesn't define you.

4. Watch the emotion ebb and flow, like a wave crashing against a shore. Remember that no feeling lasts forever.

5. Once you have made peace with your emotion and accepted its existence, you can undertake some gentle investigation. Your task here isn't to berate yourself, merely to understand what triggered it. Ask yourself:

"What was I thinking about before this emotion came along?"

"What was I doing?"

"Have I made any judgments about myself or others that prompted these feelings?"

"Beyond accepting my feelings, do I actually need to do anything about this situation?"

This exercise gives you breathing room. It lets you step back from your emotions and realize that they don't have to suck you in. Negative people tend to take their own thoughts very seriously. When you overcome this tendency, you'll find that life begins to feel much lighter. It's not that we should – or can – get rid of all negative thoughts, just that we need to learn to sit with them if we want to enjoy better psychological health.

Mindfulness Exercise: Name It, Tame It

This practice puts some distance between you and your emotions. It's simple and quick and can have profound results.[110]

1. When you feel a negative emotion swirling inside of you, stop and pause. Take a few deep breaths.

2. As you feel each emotion, label it, speaking aloud. For example, "Sad, angry, frustrated."
3. As you label each feeling, acknowledge it. Give it space. Let yourself feel detached from it. You may need to label the feeling several times, taking deep breaths in between each repetition.

Remember, all feelings will pass eventually, whatever you do.

THE DANGERS OF EMOTIONAL CONTAGION

Do you know someone who makes your heart sink whenever they enter the room? Do you have a friend or relative who always leaves you feeling negative, dissatisfied, or even depressed after just a few minutes in their company?

This phenomenon is called "emotional contagion." Along with our own emotional responses to the things that happen in our lives, we also have to learn how to handle other peoples' feelings. Otherwise, we can find ourselves at the mercy of their moods. If you work with a negative person, your emotional wellbeing will suffer unless you shield yourself from their feelings.

Mindfulness helps us respond to people around us in a sensitive and caring way, without getting caught up in their emotions. The first step is to work out who in your life is bringing you down.

Mindfulness Exercise: How Does This Person Make You Feel?

The next time you meet up with someone, whether it's a friend, relative, or coworker, check in with your body before and after your time together. Compare how you were feeling before your conversation and how you feel after spending time together.

Does your body feel more or less tense? Is your breathing slower or faster? Are your thoughts mostly positive or negative? Do you feel more or less enthusiastic about life in general?

Repeat this exercise, with different people, several times over the course of a few weeks. You'll start to notice that some people leave you feeling energized and positive, whereas others drain your spirit. You don't need to do anything with this information yet; just adopt the role of observer.

HOW TO RESPOND TO OTHER PEOPLES' NEGATIVITY

Staying mindful when you're dealing with someone else takes practice, but it can be done. Try to stop taking everything personally. Realize that, for the most part, someone else's bad mood has nothing to do with you.

Psychologist David J. Pollay calls this the "Law of the Garbage Truck." He points out that most people carry around a host of problems and bring their negative attitude wherever they go. If you aren't careful, they will happily dump it on you or anyone else who comes along.[111]

The next time someone starts trying to offload their negativity onto you, smile and deflect the conversation elsewhere. Remind yourself that you don't have to accept their garbage.

At the same time, remember that you never know the full story. It's possible that one of their relatives is sick or that they are facing major stress at work. Try to give them the benefit of the doubt.

You can also create a "pause policy." If someone sends you an email or text that stirs up difficult, negative feelings in you, wait at least an hour (if possible) before responding. Give yourself a chance to sit with your emotions, and give yourself time to think of a positive response.

SPEND LESS TIME WITH NEGATIVE PEOPLE

Mindfully choosing to recognize and deal with negativity will make you considerably happier. If you have to work or live with negative people, you have no other choice if you want more peace and less stress in your life.

On the other hand, you might want to think about spending less time with negative people. For example, you can't order your coworkers to leave your company, but you can reduce the amount of time you spend with toxic friends and acquaintances.

Being mindful doesn't mean you have to tolerate bad behavior. If the people in your life drag you down, it might be time to make a few changes. Focus instead on surrounding yourself with people who make you feel peaceful, happy to be alive, and accepted for who you are.

It may come as a shock to realize that those closest to you are draining your energy. Moving toward a more mindful life can be tough because it involves facing unpleasant truths about your relationships, and this can be painful. Just by paying attention to your body and feelings, you'll quickly realize who is worthy of your time, and who treats you like a garbage disposal plant.

GRATITUDE & NEGATIVITY

Negative people focus on what is going wrong in their lives, which creates a sense of dissatisfaction. This is why gratitude practices are useful if you're trying to kick the negativity habit.

This exercise is based on something you do every day, which makes it easy to slot into your regular routine.

Mindfulness Exercise: Grateful "Thank you's"

Over the course of an average day, many of us say "thank you" several times. For example, you probably say "Thanks" when a colleague makes you a coffee or when your partner cleans up after dinner. But do you feel grateful when you say thank you, or has it become somewhat automatic?

The next time you say thank you, pay attention to why you are thanking the other person and take the opportunity to feel gratitude. For example, if your partner does the dishes, take a few seconds to be grateful that they are willing to pitch in with day-to-day chores. If your friend gets you a coffee, take a moment to feel grateful that you get to spend time with a kind, generous person.[112]

If you aren't going to say "thank you" to anyone in the near future, you can try the next practice instead.

Mindfulness Exercise: Take Five

When you next feel frustrated or overwhelmed, grab a piece of paper and write down five things you are grateful for. If you aren't sure where to start, just take a look around. Do you have access to washing facilities? Clean water? Nutritious food? That's three things right there. With a little effort, you'll be able to think of dozens more.

Do you feel reluctant or angry when you try this exercise? That's okay. Maybe you can't help focusing on what's going wrong in your life. Perhaps you think that a gratitude exercise can't possibly make you feel any better, or that everything is too hard and there is nothing to be thankful for.

Do it anyway. It only takes five minutes, and what have you got to lose? Give it a few tries; studies have proven that gratitude practices help most people feel better. Psychologists have found that grateful people are happier and more hopeful, and people who take time to reminisce about fond memories tend to be more content.[113]

Mindfulness & Emotional Intelligence

Mindfulness enhances your emotional intelligence, or EQ. People with high EQs are skilled in identifying and handling their feelings. They are also adept at picking up on other people's emotions and cheering them up if they're feeling low. By learning how to face and sit with your negative emotions, you'll be able to acknowledge and deal with tough situations and setbacks.

Emotionally intelligent people are more likely to take risks because they know they can handle fear and disappointment. They go beyond their comfort zones and embrace challenge and change. Just think how your career and relationships would change if you no longer felt afraid of fear itself.

Research shows a clear link between mindfulness, EQ, positive mood, and life satisfaction.[114] Psychologists believe that mindful people are more aware of their moods, which helps them choose how best to handle them.

Facing up to your own feelings can also help you channel them in a healthy way. For example, if you are mindful of your own feelings, you might decide that a workout would help you let go of your anger.[115] You'll start making healthier choices, which will have a powerful knock-on effect in every area of your life.

SUMMARY

- Some stress can be a positive force, but too much is a health risk.
- Mindfulness helps you monitor your body and mind for signs of stress, prompting you to face the problem before it gets out of hand.
- Mindfulness can protect you against burnout.
- Sitting with, and accepting your negative emotions can make them seem less overwhelming.
- Mindfulness helps shield you from other people's negativity.
- Cultivating mindfulness will automatically improve your EQ because you will learn how to tune into your feelings.

CHAPTER 5:

MINDFULNESS & ANGER MANAGEMENT

T here's nothing wrong with getting angry, or even furious, when the situation warrants it. Anger inspires us to defend ourselves and correct injustice. However, too much anger takes its toll on your mind, body, and relationships.

If you have an anger problem, mindfulness practice will help you learn how to spot the warning signs that your anger is spinning out of control.

ANGER DOESN'T ALWAYS COME FROM THE OUTSIDE

The commonsense view is that anger is triggered by external events. For example, if you think you lost your job for no reason other than your boss dislikes you, you may be angry. If someone cuts you off in traffic, you may feel mad.

However, anger can also stem from a loss of joy. Psychologist Stephen Dansiger, who specializes in anger management, points out that no mood state is permanent. It's unrealistic to expect that we can be happy or relaxed all the time. Unfortunately, some people find this hard to accept, and their disappointment may manifest itself as frustration or anger.[116] Dansiger notes that these individuals feel a sense of loss when feelings of contentment or joy pass, especially if they have a generally unhappy disposition, and this manifests as irritability.

So, How Does Mindfulness Help?

Mindfulness helps you check in with your body, detect the early signs of anger, and respond to the situation in a way that doesn't harm you or others.

Mindfulness Exercise: How Angry Are You?

If you know or suspect that you have an anger management problem, start by checking in with yourself every two to three hours. All you need to do is set aside a couple of minutes to tune into your mind and body.

Ask yourself the following questions:

1. On a scale of 1-10, with 10 representing an extreme level of anger, how angry am I right now?
2. How does my body feel?
3. What emotions am I feeling right now?
4. What thoughts are going through my head?

This practice helps you detach from your emotions, which makes it easier to remain calm. Remember, anger itself isn't the problem; it's when we start identifying with our anger that we run into trouble.

Mindfulness Exercise: RAIN

This practice, developed by teacher Michele McDonald, can be used to handle any difficult emotion. It is especially useful for taming anger.

RAIN stands for Recognize, Allow, Investigate, and Nurture.

1. **Recognize:** Begin by giving yourself permission to feel your anger. Label it. If you are alone, speak aloud. Tell yourself, "I am angry." Scan your body; do you notice any sensations that signal anger? For example, is your breathing shallow? Have you curled your hands into fists?

2. **Allow:** Hold your anger. Let it just be there. Don't try to reason it away. Whatever your thoughts and feelings, accept them exactly as they are. If you can sit with your anger, you'll learn that it doesn't have to overwhelm you.

3. **Investigate:** Only after you've recognized and felt your anger can you explore what triggered it. Take an attitude of gentle curiosity; there's no need to beat yourself up for being angry. Ask what happened immediately before you feel fury bubble up inside you.

   You don't have to make psychological breakthroughs every time you do the RAIN exercise but, over time, you'll start noticing your personal anger patterns. For example, you might notice that you are quick to get angry when you think someone has failed to respect your authority.

   Discovering your triggers gives you an advantage. Depending on the situation, you might be able to avoid triggers, but in most cases, you will need to learn how to work with them. This may mean challenging your assumptions (e.g. "Everyone should respect my authority at all times, and if they don't, it's terrible!") or working on your emotional intelligence (e.g. learning to be more patient towards others.)

4. **Nurture:** Anger is often a sign that your needs are going unmet. For instance, suppose you are angry because your mother doesn't seem interested when you tell her about the problems you are having in your marriage. Your anger may stem from the fact that she isn't offering the kind of nurturing parental love that you want and need.

    However angry you may be, you deserve self-compassion, not condemnation. You also need to learn how to nurture yourself when others cannot or will not provide you with love and support. Self-care is an essential part of the RAIN exercise. Have a bath or shower, do some exercise, mindfully eat your favorite food, or do something else that makes you feel good. Congratulate yourself for taking responsibility for your feelings.

Any Progress Is Great!

If you frequently get angry, cut yourself some slack when you do these exercises. Your anger won't disappear immediately. You'll probably still feel frustrated, even when the most intense emotions have passed. That's OK. Getting angry is a learned behavior, and changing an old habit is difficult. You deserve lots of praise for trying a new approach.

Get Mindful About Your Thought Patterns

Mindfulness gives you the space to play detective, and this can be really useful in understanding your personal anger patterns. The next time you get angry, watch your thoughts. Remember, you don't have to argue with them or wish them away. Reframe them; instead of things that make your life difficult, try to see your thoughts as clues to your anger patterns.[117]

Do you notice any of the following thoughts pop up when you get angry?

Blaming: Do you shift responsibility onto other people? For instance, do you catch yourself saying things like "It's her fault" or "He always makes me mad"?

The truth is that no one can "make" you mad. You have a choice. You can respond to a situation mindfully and handle your anger in a mindful way. You do not have to identify with your anger.

Over-generalizing: Do you use words like "never" or "always"? For example, do you say things like "You never listen to what I have to say" or "You always try to bring me down"?

These statements are rarely true, and they only escalate the tension between you and someone else. Be mindful of the language you use. If you have a problem with someone else's behavior, identify exactly how they are triggering your anger.

Using "should": Do you feel as though people should act fairly towards you at all times? Do you think they have a duty to always act reasonably, to always include you in their activities, and to value your opinion?

Although this would be nice, it just isn't how the world works. "Shoulding" will keep you miserable and trapped by your own unrealistic expectations.

Mind-reading: Do you assume that you "just know" what someone else is thinking? Do you catch yourself thinking things like "I know that he gets angry with me" or "I know that she doesn't think I'm up to the job"?

Unless someone tells us exactly what they're thinking, it's dangerous to assume that we know what's going through their minds. Assumptions can lead to unnecessary argument and misunderstandings.

Don't beat yourself up if you notice yourself blaming, over-generalizing, "shoulding," or mind-reading. Everyone falls into these traps sometimes. The trick is to spot your thinking errors and realize that you don't have to identify with them. Instead, you can choose to use tools like RAIN to respond in a healthier way.

GRUDGES, PAST HURTS, & RELEASING ANGER

So far, we've looked at how you can use mindfulness to deal with angry outbursts and isolated events that make you see red. But what about grudges and long-term grievances? It's worth addressing old hurts because they can cause needless pain for decades if left to fester.

Mindfulness Practice: Using Mindful Visualization To Release Anger

This exercise helps you let go of simmering resentment. You can use it as a tool for forgiveness, or simply as a way of releasing frustration and rage when your anger flares up.

1. Find a quiet place where you will be undistracted for several minutes.

2. Close your eyes and imagine a peaceful scene, preferably outdoors. You could choose a meadow, a forest, or a beach.

3. When an angry thought pops up, imagine encasing it inside a large pink bubble. Visualize the thought inside the bubble. Feel a sense of relief as you realize that it can't harm you.

4. Picture the bubble floating off into the sky until it is out of sight.

BE WILLING TO SEE CHANGE IN OTHER PEOPLE

Living in the present helps you make a fresh start in your relationships because you can see someone as they are now, not as a shadowy figure who hurt you in the past. People can and do change. You've decided to change by picking up this book and taking steps toward a more mindful life, so you know it's true!

Sometimes, someone will suddenly develop an interest in personal development, often after a major transition like an illness or milestone birthday. Others change gradually over time. They might mellow with age, or slowly shift their priorities and goals.

Either way, try to stay open to the possibility of reconciliation. This doesn't mean you have to forgive and forget. Neither does it mean you should rekindle a relationship with someone who has abused or mistreated you. In some cases, it's best to cut all contact forever. On the other hand, if your grievance is relatively minor and a lot of time has passed, why not try casting your assumptions aside?

WHEN TO SEEK HELP

These exercises can go a long way to resolving pathological anger, but they are no substitute for professional help. If your anger is disrupting your relationships or career, it's best to make an appointment with a doctor or therapist as soon as possible. Most mental health professionals are happy to use mindfulness as part of a treatment plan, so you'll be able to combine these practices with other interventions.

SUMMARY

- Anger is not an intrinsically bad emotion, but too much can harm you and those around you.
- Mindfulness practices can help you identify anger in your body, accept it, and release it.
- Identifying your personal anger patterns can help you overcome thinking errors.
- Staying mindful can help you appreciate positive change in other people.
- You can use mindfulness when working with a mental health professional who specializes in anger management.

CHAPTER 6:

DEPRESSION & MINDFULNESS

D epression is a complex illness. It can be caused by genetics, upbringing, and negative life events, but each case is unique. However, despite their differences, people diagnosed with depression seem to think in similar ways. Their thought patterns are unhelpful and destructive, keeping them locked in a cycle of misery.

According to the National Health Service (NHS), symptoms of depression include:[118]

- Low mood or sadness
- Feeling hopeless and helpless
- Low self-esteem
- Feeling guilt-ridden
- Feeling irritable and intolerant of others
- Having no motivation or interest in things
- Finding it difficult to make decisions

You may also notice physical symptoms, such as aches and pains, and social symptoms, such as a reluctance to spend time with family and friends.

Depression can be classified as "mild," "moderate," or "severe." The more severe your depression, the greater its impact on your daily functioning.

THE LINK BETWEEN THOUGHTS & MOODS

You don't have to believe everything you think. You have the power to start seeing thoughts for what they are – just thoughts – and making healthier choices that help you build a happier life.

Professor Mark Williams, a mindfulness expert and previous director of the Oxford-based Mindfulness Center, puts it this way:

"Gradually, we can train ourselves to notice when our thoughts are taking over and realize that thoughts are simply 'mental events' that do not have to control us."[119]

AARON BECK & COGNITIVE THERAPY

Back in the 1960s, a psychiatrist called Aaron T. Beck was researching depression. He was interested in how his depressed patients thought, not just how they felt. He realized that depressed people tended to:

• Have negative thoughts about themselves
• Have negative thoughts about the world
• Have negative thoughts about the future[120]

His research with depressed people made one thing clear – your thoughts shape your mood. Just like the Buddha, Beck found that when people get caught up in their thoughts and emotional reactions, they are at risk of slipping into an anxious, tense, or otherwise uncomfortable state of mind.

AARON BECK'S APPROACH TO DEALING WITH NEGATIVE THOUGHTS

Beck believed that depressed people needed to challenge their unhelpful thoughts. His logic went like this: If holding negative thoughts keeps depression going, then replacing them with new, more realistic thoughts should help improve a person's mood.

Beck invented a new form of therapy, Cognitive Therapy (CT), to help his patients fight back against their unhelpful thoughts. He worked with them to uncover their irrational thinking and replace their unhelpful thoughts with more positive statements.

For example, a CT therapist might ask their client to record the thoughts that went through their mind the last time they felt their mood take a dive. The client might record the thought, "Nothing I ever do is good enough." As Aaron Beck would point out, this is an example of a negative thought about the self.

Once the client had identified this thought, the therapist would then work with them to challenge it, using logic and reason. For instance, they might help the client think of times they have succeeded in meeting challenges. The therapist and client might work to come up with a new belief, such as "I am capable of succeeding sometimes, and my work is often good enough."

Critics of CT say that the average person has so many thoughts throughout the day that it's unrealistic to expect them to challenge each and every one. There is no agreement among CT therapists on how many times you need to challenge them before you can expect to see improvement. What's more, if you are depressed, you might not have the mental energy to argue with your thoughts.

THE MINDFUL ALTERNATIVE

Mindfulness practitioners agree that our thoughts do maintain our emotional states. They also agree that depressed people usually think in particular ways. However, they disagree with Beck on one key point. Instead of just challenging unhelpful thoughts, they believe depressed people also need to learn how to sit with unpleasant feelings.

We're going to look at how mindfulness practices can help alleviate the symptoms of depression. You'll find that other chapters in this book indirectly address symptoms not covered here. For example, irritability is a common sign of depression, so you may find the chapter on anger management useful.

Depression sucks the joy from almost all situations. For instance, you might be spending time with your partner or kids, but feel very little joy. This makes you feel even more depressed. You start thinking, "If I can't even enjoy these special times, what's the point in carrying on?"

Mindfulness exercises can put you back in touch with your own capacity to experience excitement and pleasure. This starts an upwards spiral; you remember what joy feels like, which inspires you to keep trying to find happiness in everyday situations, which makes you happier, and so on. All the exercises in this book will help you find your way back to the present moment and, as a result, increase your pleasure in living.

Please note: Although mindfulness has been shown to help with symptoms of depression, these practices are not a substitute for personalized medical advice or treatment. If you are depressed or suspect you have depression, work with your regular doctor or therapist to treat your condition.

DEPRESSION, CONCENTRATION, & FOCUS

An inability to concentrate is a common symptom of depression. Sufferers find it difficult to read books, follow TV shows, complete tasks at work, or even take part in everyday conversations.

It's not merely a nuisance; it's downright scary when your brain is wrapped in a thick fog. This is why many depressed people retreat from the world. Even when they want to take part in activities, they often feel cut off from everyone, which itself is depressing.

Fortunately, mindfulness has been proven to enhance concentration. For example, research shows that practicing mindfulness regularly for only 7 weeks is likely to improve your attention span, which can make a big difference in your quality of life.[121]

The following practice is a great way to train your attention span. Do it for a few minutes every day, and you should notice improvements quickly.

Mindfulness Exercise: Counting To 10

1. Sit or lie down in a comfortable position.
2. Take a few deep breaths in and out, keeping your attention on your breathing.
3. As you breathe in, count "One."
4. As you exhale, count "Two."
5. Continue until you reach "Ten."
6. If you notice your mind wandering off, bring it back to the present, and start over.

This sounds simple, but it may take a lot of practice before you can count all the way up to ten. Stick with it. Within a few days, it will start to get easier.

DEPRESSION, GRATITUDE, & "COUNTING YOUR BLESSINGS"

When you're depressed, the world is a bleak place. You might find that you focus on the suffering you see around you or the upsetting stories you hear on the news. Gratitude practices affirm that there is still hope and kindness, even when everything feels unbearable. They can inspire moments of peace and even joy, however fleeting.

Don't confuse this with the old cliché, "count your blessings." There's a subtle yet important distinction here.

Counting your blessings usually means rattling off a list of things and people in your life, whereas gratitude practice entails slowing down and mindfully appreciating your resources and relationships. People tell you to count your blessings as a means of just brushing off difficulties and struggles. Mindfulness is the opposite; it enables you to accept whatever is going on in your life.

What's more, gratitude practice doesn't involve guilt. You don't need to beat yourself up for being unhappy with your life or wanting to make changes. All you need to do is show up, sit quietly, and acknowledge what you have. Being grateful doesn't mean that you stop noticing your problems, and it definitely isn't a cure for depression. However, it is an effective tool that can help you lead a more mindful life.

Mindfulness Exercise: Gratitude

Start by reflecting on the positive things in your life. Think small. Give thanks for the clean water in your glass, the shoes on your feet, and so on.

Next, reflect on things that are not necessarily good, but may offer you opportunities for growth. For example, you may have been facing problems at work, but your difficulties might encourage you to search for a new, more satisfying position.

Skeptical? When you're depressed, that's understandable. You might be encouraged to know that research shows gratitude exercises can make a big difference. Gratitude reduces feelings of depression, boosts overall wellbeing, and improves sleep quality.[122] You'll feel the benefits within a couple of sessions.

Mindfulness, Acceptance, & Releasing Guilt

If you've ever had depression, you're probably all too familiar with the following phrases:

"What have you got to be depressed about?"

"Count your blessings!"

"There are people out there with real problems. Get over yourself."

This kind of "advice" doesn't help. It actually worsens the situation, because it makes you feel guilty for feeling depressed in the first place. Depression can also make you feel guilty because it encourages you to think about the past. You quickly find yourself getting mad at your past self.

Mindfulness teaches you to accept your depression for what it is. Having depression doesn't make you a bad or ungrateful person. It means you are struggling with a mental health problem that affects millions of people. Through mindfulness, you can gain insight into your thought processes and come to acknowledge that they have no bearing on your worth as a person.

To recover from depression, you need to show yourself some compassion. If you are battling negative thoughts and feel bad about yourself on a daily basis, this is a big challenge! The good news is that it becomes easier with practice.

A Mindfulness Exercise For Self-Compassion

This is a quick, simple practice for those times you are tempted to judge yourself harshly.[123]

1. When you catch yourself thinking self-critical thoughts, make a conscious decision to pause.
2. Decide that you are going to take a few moments to be mindful.
3. Gently place your hand over your heart.
4. Slowly take a few breaths. Watch your breathing. If your mind continues to chatter away, just watch it. Avoid arguing with it.
5. Let yourself feel emotional pain. Acknowledge that you are suffering.

When you are in the depths of depression, trying to do this exercise whenever you judge yourself isn't realistic because depressed people put themselves down with alarming frequency. Just try your best. Aim to do it a few times per day.

Depression & Your Self-Image

Depressed people don't feel good about themselves. If you have a nasty inner critic, it's hard to appreciate yourself. That horrible little voice will highlight all of your supposed flaws and mistakes. A poor self-image and low self-esteem helps keep the cycle of depression going. When you see yourself as a terrible person, you'll conclude that you aren't worthy of time or help.

Depression makes you see the world through a grey filter. You stop appreciating or even noticing the things you do well, and dwell on the bad stuff instead. Over time, you start constructing an image of yourself as inferior and flawed. Mindfulness can help break the cycle by giving you a healthy degree of distance from your emotions.

Practicing the self-compassion exercise above can help because it encourages self-acceptance. The following exercise works in a different way, by capturing your negative self-talk and helping you detach yourself from it.

Mindfulness Exercise: "I'm Having The Thought That…"

The next time you notice a self-deprecating thought, add, "I'm having the thought that…" in front of it.

For instance, if you catch yourself thinking, "I'm so lazy, I'll never get anything done," tell yourself, "I'm having the thought that I'm so lazy and I'll never get anything done." The thought may or may not disappear, but you'll have achieved your objective – it won't feel quite so personal. Remember, don't try to argue with the thought. Your mission is to notice, reframe, and sit with it.

As you continue on with your mindfulness journey, your self-esteem will gradually start to improve. Taking responsibility for yourself is empowering. Knowing that you are taking steps to boost your quality of life will bolster your self-image as someone in control of their destiny.

Preventing Relapse With Mindfulness-Based Cognitive Therapy (MBCT)

Mindfulness-Based Cognitive Therapy (MBCT) is an extension of traditional CT. It helps people recognize unhelpful thinking styles and learn to accept and explore them without judgment. MBCT is particularly useful for people who have had three or more previous episodes of depression.[124]

Zindel Segal, one of the founders of MBCT, points out that depression has a tendency to come back. Whereas CT practitioners focus on helping a client move on from their current period of depression, MBCT has been specially designed to help them stay well.

According to Segal, people who have recovered from depression are easily triggered to relapse when they experience a sad mood or negative thoughts. Depression appears to sensitize the brain to further episodes.

The answer? By staying mindful to shifts in mood and negative thoughts, people can prevent themselves from spiraling into another episode. MBCT techniques aren't designed to stop people from feeling sad, because ups and downs are a normal part of life. Instead, MBCT helps people learn to accept their emotions.[125]

MBCT EXERCISES

MBCT is usually taught as an eight-week group therapy program. However, you can still enjoy the benefits by practicing MBCT exercises by yourself.

MBCT Exercise #1: The 3-Minute Breathing Space

As the name implies, this exercise takes three minutes. You could set a timer on your phone to chime every sixty seconds. The practice can stand alone, or it makes a good "warm-up" exercise for a longer mindfulness training session.

During the first minute, ask yourself this question: "How am I right now?" Notice any sensations, feelings, and thoughts that arise in your mind and body.

During the second minute, simply follow your breath. Notice the rise and fall of your chest. Notice the temperature of the air.

During the final minute, move your attention from your breath outwards so that you are noticing sensations throughout your body.

MBCT Exercise #2: Mindful Dishwashing

Washing the dishes is an excellent opportunity to use all your senses and ground yourself in the moment. As you wash a plate, notice how the water and soap feel against your skin. Look at how the water and suds slide around the plate, and how the sponge or cloth removes the debris. Hear the sloshing of the water. You may be able to smell or taste the scent or perfume of detergent in the air. With practice, this mundane task can become a rewarding part of your day.

SUMMARY

- If you are suffering from depression, you probably experience a lot of negative thoughts about yourself and the world.
- Some therapists believe that challenging these thoughts is important, but mindfulness practitioners believe that learning to accept them is more effective.
- Mindfulness-Based Cognitive Therapy (MBCT) works by reducing rumination and preventing the kind of downward spiral that can lead to depression.
- Mindfulness can also help people with depression release guilt and shame, grow their self-compassion, improve their self-image, and enjoy brief moments of pleasure.

CHAPTER 7:

MINDFULNESS EXERCISES FOR ANXIETY & PANIC ATTACKS

People who can keep their attention on the present moment rarely experience anxiety. They acknowledge that the future may be unpleasant, but they aren't caught up in the pain of anticipating it. They are free to appreciate the present. Mindfulness training can reduce worry and fear.[126]

In this chapter, you'll learn how mindfulness can help you cope with the symptoms of anxiety. Note that mindfulness in general is good for anyone suffering from anxiety disorders. However, the techniques in this chapter are especially effective for people who feel too anxious to even attempt mindfulness exercises. We'll also look at how mindfulness can help you deal with panic attacks.

What Is Anxiety?

Anxiety is a feeling of fear, worry, or general unease. Some anxiety is normal and healthy. If we didn't get anxious about potentially dangerous situations or serious problems, we might not prepare for them properly. For example, feeling anxious before an important test can give you an edge and help you get a better grade.

On the other hand, chronic or severe anxiety wreaks havoc on your body and mind. If your anxiety starts affecting your life – for example, if you are so worried or nervous that you can't get your work done – you may have an anxiety disorder. Psychological symptoms of excessive anxiety include being irritable, feeling uneasy most of the time, difficulty sleeping, feeling as though you could cry at any moment, and seeking more reassurance than usual from other people. You may also experience physical symptoms, such as feeling faint, a loss of appetite, an upset stomach, headaches, and palpitations.

CAN YOU BE TOO ANXIOUS TO PRACTICE MINDFULNESS?

If you are very anxious, mindfulness might feel completely impossible. For example, you may try to sit down and observe your breathing for a few moments, but feel your anxiety rising until it feels unbearable. Self-critical thoughts, such as "I can't do this right" and "This is just making me too worried" start creeping in.

Fortunately, you can ease yourself into mindfulness by working on self-compassion. Psychologist Mitch Ablett suggests that people with high anxiety can use the following practice as a bridge to meditation and other mindfulness exercises.[127]

Mindfulness Exercise: Self-Compassion Mindfulness For Anxiety

1. Sit upright in a comfortable chair. It doesn't matter whether you keep your eyes closed or open.
2. Acknowledge that you are suffering from anxiety. Tell yourself out loud, "I'm acknowledging that I'm in a lot of emotional pain. My suffering is real."

3. Take a single deep breath. Notice how it feels to inhale then exhale.
4. Affirm your pain again. This time, say "I'm caring for myself."
5. Repeat step #3, but this time focus on two breathing cycles.
6. Tell yourself, "This is hard for me. I accept that."
7. Try to observe three breathing cycles.
8. Again, acknowledge that the practice is challenging. Tell yourself that your pain is real and that your practice is a form of self-care.

Repeat this practice as many times as you like. At first, completing it once will be tough, and that's okay. A few minutes is all you need. After a few sessions, you'll begin to notice the difference.

Showing self-compassion is a great first step when you have anxiety. The next practice uses drawing as a grounding exercise. If you struggle to remain still during your mindfulness sessions, it's a great alternative to conventional seated practices.

Mindfulness Exercise: Drawing Mandalas

You've probably seen mandala coloring books for adults, or even tried one yourself. Their creators claim that coloring the patterns is relaxing and can relieve stress and anxiety. Buddhists would agree; the ancient practice of drawing and coloring mandalas has long been used as a form of meditation.[128]

Mandalas are abstract designs, usually circular, made up of geometric forms, organic shapes, or both. They can be left plain or colored. A mandala has an identifiable central point.

Their shapes and forms radiate outward. In Sanskrit, the word "mandala" means "circle."

Follow these steps to draw your own mandalas:

1. Find a square piece of paper. It can be whatever size you like.
2. Draw a small dot in the center of the paper. You can use a ruler to check the positioning.
3. Draw three or four concentric circles. Every circle should have the dot at its center.
4. Let your intuition guide you when drawing your mandala. The only rule is that it should be symmetrical. Mandalas are repetitive, which is one reason they are psychologically soothing. Keep the colors symmetrical too.
5. You can add color as you go, or wait until you have completed your design before adding it.
6. As you draw, notice the sensation of the pencil or pen in your hand. Notice how lines and color appear on the page. What does it feel like to make contact with the paper?

If you make a mistake, don't beat yourself up. You don't need to produce a perfect work of art; the aim is to focus your attention on the act of drawing. When you are engrossed in creating a mandala, your mind is less likely to stray to thoughts that make you anxious.

You may even experience a flow state whilst drawing and coloring. During a flow state, you become completely engrossed in whatever you are doing. You forget where you are, and time seems to fly by. You never have to watch the clock, and your mind effortlessly focuses on the task in front of you.

By definition, you can't force yourself into a flow state. See it as a nice side-effect rather than a goal, and simply appreciate it.

MINDFULNESS FOR PANIC ATTACKS

Panic attacks are overwhelming with sudden feelings of anxiety combined with physical symptoms. During an attack, your body releases stress hormones, including cortisol and adrenaline. These cause symptoms like nausea, irregular breathing, palpitations, sweating, and lightheadedness. Panic attacks last up to half an hour, but most peak within ten minutes. They sometimes have a clear trigger, but they can also happen for no obvious reason.

The good news is that panic attacks aren't harmful. Unfortunately, if you don't learn how to handle them, they can start to take over your life. For example, if you experience a panic attack, you might start to worry about suffering further attacks in the future. Ironically, this can make them more likely to happen, and the cycle continues.

Mindful approaches to panic attacks are becoming more popular among mental health professionals. Instead of distracting yourself from an attack, try sitting with – or even embracing – the sensations.

Mindfulness Exercise: Sitting With A Panic Attack

1. The next time you detect the beginnings of a panic attack, pause and take a deep breath. Tell yourself, "Ah, here we go. This is a panic attack."

2. Remind yourself that your symptoms always pass.

3. Adopt an attitude of curiosity rather than resistance. Notice your physical symptoms. Label them. For example, "sweaty palms," "chest tightness," and so on.

4. Watch your symptoms reach their peak. Usually, this will be at the ten-minute mark.

This exercise will help you accept what is happening in your body. When you decide to experience a panic attack instead of reacting with more panic, it might even pass more quickly than usual.

Mindfulness Exercise: Say "STOP!"

Here's an exercise you can do whenever you start feeling overwhelmed by worry. With practice, you can use it to delay panic attacks or prevent them entirely.

STOP stands for Slow down, Take a breath, Observe, and Proceed.[129]

1. Stop. Whatever you are doing, pause. Move away from your desk, put your phone down, or find someplace to sit.

2. Take a breath. If you are experiencing racing thoughts, say "In" with each inhalation, and "Out" every time you exhale.

3. Observe. Consider how your body feels. Label your emotions. Step back and notice the thoughts racing through your head. Remember that your thoughts and feelings don't always represent reality.

4. Proceed. Pick an activity that will give you a psychological boost. For example, you could call a friend for support or make yourself a hot drink.

Befriending Anxiety

Harvard psychology professor Ron Siegel recommends that people with anxiety go one step further. He says that not only should you learn how to "ride out" waves of anxiety, but actually induce it. By deliberately triggering anxious feelings, you can practice letting them pass through you. This exercise is powerful because it teaches you that all anxiety passes eventually.

Mindfulness Exercise: Inducing Anxiety[130]

1. Sit quietly and scan your body for signs of tension or anxiety.
2. If you can locate any feelings of anxiety, such as a knot in your stomach, allow yourself to notice it.
3. If not, intentionally bring to mind a situation or person who makes you afraid or worried. Choose something that makes you apprehensive rather than terrified.
4. Breathe deeply and acknowledge your fear.
5. It won't be long before your mind wanders off. When this happens, return to the anxious feeling. You'll soon notice that maintaining a state of anxiety is actually quite difficult. Even when you want it to stick around, it fades within a few minutes.

Working With Your Doctor

Mindfulness definitely works well for lots of people who have to deal with anxiety. On the other hand, it's not a cure-all. You'll need to make lifestyle changes and possibly work with a doctor or therapist to make a full recovery. Eating a good diet, getting plenty of exercise, and working on your relationships usually make up the other pieces of the puzzle.

If your symptoms are having a major impact on your life, or self-help measures don't appear to be working, it's time to consult a mental health professional. Your regular physician will be able to point you in the right direction. Doctors and therapists are starting to appreciate the power of mindfulness, so they will probably be happy to help you incorporate it as part of a treatment plan.

Summary

- Mindfulness grounds you in the present, so it is useful for anyone who worries and ruminates.
- Mindful drawing is a longstanding tradition that can alleviate anxiety and stress.
- Mindfulness can help you cope with a panic attack because it has a grounding effect.
- Mindfully inducing anxiety teaches you that anxiety doesn't last forever. This is an empowering concept.
- If you are too anxious to try mindfulness practices, acknowledging this anxiety can be a great help.
- If anxiety is interfering with your life and self-help isn't working, consult a doctor.

CHAPTER 8:

BUILDING BETTER HABITS WITH MINDFULNESS

Never underestimate the power of habit. Much of our day-to-day lives, including the thoughts we have about ourselves and others, are shaped by repetition. The more you repeat a habit, the harder it is to shake.

In this chapter, we'll look at how you can conquer undesirable habits using mindfulness. We'll also talk about ways you can use mindfulness to build new, healthy habits that will help you meet your life goals.

Not all habits are harmful. Brushing your teeth in the morning is a habit, as is washing your hands after you use the bathroom. Good habits keep you aligned with your higher goals and objectives. In this case, tooth brushing and handwashing steer you on the right path to your goal of leading a healthy life. It's only when our habits prevent us from fulfilling our potential that they become a problem.

OVERCOMING "BAD" HABITS

We all know what we mean when we talk about "bad habits." Smoking, drinking too much, watching too much TV, and interrupting others are common examples. The problem with this phrase is that it invites judgment. By labeling a behavior as "bad," we're affirming to ourselves that our behavior is fundamentally wrong. This isn't a helpful way to talk to ourselves, because it triggers self-criticism. And, as we know, criticizing ourselves isn't constructive.[131]

Instead, refer to habits that disrupt your life or stop you achieving your goals as "unhelpful" or "unhealthy." It may seem like a subtle difference, but changing your vocabulary encourages a more compassionate attitude, which can help you choose healthier habits. Unhealthy habits don't make you a bad person. We all have them!

Mindfulness Exercise: Identifying Unhealthy Habits

The first step to conquering unhealthy habits is to identify them. Over the next few days, make a note whenever you catch yourself engaging in habit-driven behavior that doesn't align with your values. For instance, if you value efficiency and achievement, compulsively checking your email every ten minutes is an unhelpful habit that doesn't serve you.

Ask yourself how you feel when you engage in this habit. Do you feel physical discomfort, emotional discomfort, or both? Pretend you are a scientist or anthropologist. Act as a neutral witness rather than a critic. How does this habit prevent you from leading the kind of life you want to live?

Some habits, such as smoking, are always harmful. However, other habits don't fall into the same category. For example, consider excessive internet use and overeating. Unlike smoking, using the internet and eating are not intrinsically unhealthy behaviors. It's only when you start to abuse them that the trouble starts. You can't stop eating, and it's unrealistic to cut the internet out of your life, but you can learn to take a mindful approach and moderate your behavior.

WHY HABITS ARE SO HARD TO BREAK

So, you've identified your unhelpful habits and decided to make changes. Unfortunately, as you probably know, it isn't that easy to adopt new behaviors overnight.

To help understand why habits stick like glue, let's look at two complementary theories.

THE DUAL OPERATING SYSTEMS THEORY

Economist Daniel Kahneman has proposed that human beings have two "operating systems" when it comes to making decisions: System 1 and System 2. System 1 is driven by instinct and emotion. It urges us to take immediate action to solve a problem or relieve discomfort. For instance, if you are very thirsty, you will feel an overwhelming compulsion to drink a glass of water if it's placed in front of you.

By contrast, System 2 is based on rational thought. When System 2 takes over, we can think about the long-term effects of our actions.[132]

To put it simply, System 1 creates the urge to engage in unhealthy habits. When you try to suppress a habit, such as biting your nails or reaching for a piece of candy even though you aren't hungry, you are forced to battle against a powerful force that's hard to subdue with willpower.

Sure, you might be able to grit your teeth and fight the urge occasionally, but merely urging yourself to act differently isn't the best solution. As your habit becomes more and more entrenched, your intentions become even less effective.

System 2 relies on the prefrontal cortex, which is the part of the brain responsible for long-term planning. It's the part of your brain that recognizes the cost of indulging in an unhealthy habit or craving. However, you can't depend on your prefrontal cortex to always steer you in the right direction. When you are under stress, it shuts down. The cruel irony is that stress often makes cravings worse, so when you really need your prefrontal cortex, it's not much help.

If you think about it, this shouldn't come as a surprise. For example, perhaps you have experienced "brain freeze" during an exam or said something regrettable during a heated argument with a friend.

While the prefrontal cortex goes quiet under stress, the older parts of the human brain take over. The prefrontal cortex is a relatively recent development in human history. Before it arrives on the scene, our behaviors are controlled by parts of the brain that cause us to act on impulse. The result? When we feel threatened, whether by external or internal events, it's all too easy to give in to our urges. It's only later, when our prefrontal cortex comes back online, that we can reflect on the damage we've done.

THE REWARD CIRCUIT – TRIGGER, BEHAVIOR, REWARD

Psychologist Judson Brewer, a researcher with a special interest in addiction, points out that our brains have evolved to form habits. They operate on the principles of positive and negative reinforcement. If something feels good, you'll want to do it again. If something feels bad, your brain will try to avoid it.[133]

Let's take a simple example. One day, you see a delicious-looking piece of cake – a trigger. Your brain automatically urges you to eat it – a behavior – because it suspects that the cake will taste great. You eat the cake and it does indeed taste fantastic. These sensations are your reward for eating the cake.

Once this process is complete, your brain lays down what psychologists call a context-dependent memory. Your brain creates a new pathway that lets you remember what you just ate – cake – and where you found it. From a survival perspective, this is a wonderful mechanism because it will save you time in the future. You won't have to wonder whether cake tastes good; you'll be drawn to it straight away. This makes the cake harder to resist.

Your brain may then decide that cake may be the answer when you next feel sad, lonely, or otherwise uncomfortable. When you respond to an internal trigger – an uncomfortable feeling – and eat cake, you'll find that you do feel better, just as your brain predicted. Every time you respond to your triggers, you further cement this new habit. Over time, it starts to feel more natural and becomes harder to shift.

So, How Can We Change?

The picture might seem a bit bleak right now, but you can change! You just need to adopt a new, more mindful approach. With regular training, you can change your routine to help you make better choices, you can explore your cravings mindfully, and you can train your prefrontal cortex to help you out during stressful moments.

In brief, you need to:

1. Take a proactive approach to blocking your behaviors.
2. Take an attitude of curiosity, rather than condemnation, when you act on your impulses or cravings.

NOTICE YOUR TRIGGERS & PUT UP SOME ROADBLOCKS

Having investigated your personal triggers, you can make adjustments to your environment or routine that make it easier to practice healthier habits without having to rely on willpower alone.

Some examples:

- If you have a habit of buying candy whenever you visit the grocery store, plan a new route around the store that doesn't take you through the candy aisle.
- If you check your email and social media as soon as you wake up in the morning, start leaving your phone in the kitchen when you go to bed. Get an old-fashioned alarm clock for your bedside table so that you don't need to rely on your phone to wake you up.
- If you automatically switch on the TV as soon as you come home from work, move the TV to another room or store the remote somewhere you can't easily access it.

Persistence is key. Psychologists believe that it takes approximately 66 days to build a new habit.[134] Making big changes requires a lot of effort. Make things easier on yourself by focusing on one or two changes at a time. Don't try to reinvent yourself or your life overnight; you'll become overwhelmed and may give up completely. Remember to congratulate yourself along the way.

A feeling or thought can drive us towards an unhealthy coping mechanism, but we don't have to go along with it. You are not at the mercy of your brain.

Embrace Your Cravings

In Chapter Seven, you learned that leaning into a panic attack instead of resisting it will help your symptoms pass quicker and that deliberately triggering anxiety proves to yourself that you can handle it.

This exercise is based on the same principle.

Mindfulness Exercise: Urge Surfing[135]

1. As soon as you notice a craving or urge, stop what you are doing.

2. Sit or stand still, and get as comfortable as possible.

3. Tune into your body. Where can you feel the craving? Is your body tense? Are you sweating? Describe it in non-judgmental language. For instance, you might say to yourself, "I notice that my mouth is dry, and I am craving a beer."

   If you can't locate the urge in your body, think back to another time you experienced the craving. Close your eyes and bring the memory to life in as much detail as possible. If you are worried that recalling this memory will prompt you to give in to a craving, recall a time you felt the urge but didn't act on it.

4. Having identified the part of your body most strongly associated with your craving, pay close attention to how it feels. Do the sensations change or move around? Could you draw an outline on your body, showing where you feel this sensation?

   Notice any thoughts that pop into your head. For instance, are you trying to argue or bargain with yourself? Watch out for thoughts like "Just don't do it" or "This is terrible! I can't bear this feeling!" Sit with them.

5. Breathe as normal for 1-2 minutes.

6. Return your attention to the part of your body where you are experiencing the craving. Imagine that you are directing your breath towards it. Do the sensations change?

7. Urges tend to come and go in waves. Think of your breath as a surfboard. When a wave hits you, take a big breath in. As it passes, exhale. Tell yourself that you are an expert surfer and that riding the wave is no big deal for you.

8. Within 20-30 minutes, you'll notice that your urge has started to soften.

Believe it or not, confronting urges can become fun! Judson Brewer points out that curiosity is, in itself, rewarding. You'll start to get a kick out of sitting with your cravings, which is much more constructive than mindlessly giving into your urges or trying to white-knuckle your way through a craving.

Understanding how habits work can also help us be more compassionate and understanding of others. Now that you know how easy it is to form a habit, you might find yourself making (reasonable) allowances for their behavior. You'll be able to relate to them on a deeper level, seeing them as fallible human beings just like you.

WHEN YOU SLIP UP, SHOW YOURSELF SOME COMPASSION

You're human, and you will fall back into your old habits at some point. For example, you may have had a particularly stressful day at work, and the idea of surfing an urge for 20 minutes might seem ridiculous when you could grab a chocolate bar or smoke a cigarette instead.

It's okay to be an imperfect person. Reaffirm your commitment to making changes and aim to be mindful next time around. Mindfulness will become a healthy habit and get easier the more you practice.

SUMMARY

- Our habits dictate our behaviors and can shape our lives in profound ways.
- Our brains are hardwired to form habits, and they tend to become irrational when under stress.
- Through mindfulness and observation, we can learn to surf cravings and make simple changes to our routines that prevent them from arising in the first place.
- Try to take an attitude of curiosity rather than judgment when working with habits.
- Paying attention to your habits may not come naturally at first, but observing them will eventually become second nature.
- Show yourself compassion when you slip back into unhealthy habits.

CHAPTER 9:

BEATING PROCRASTINATION & BOOSTING PRODUCTIVITY WITH MINDFULNESS

P rocrastination isn't merely an annoyance; it can do serious damage to your career, personal life, and self-esteem. In this chapter, we'll look at what procrastination is, why we do it, and how mindfulness can help us get back on track.

WHAT EXACTLY DOES IT MEAN TO PROCRASTINATE?

When we procrastinate, we delay a task. Most people associate procrastination with school and work. None of us are surprised when a student admits that they have been procrastinating instead of studying for a test or writing an essay. At work, we might procrastinate on menial or challenging tasks, such as writing a presentation or drawing up a complex spreadsheet.

However, we also procrastinate in our personal lives. For example, some people vow to lose weight or give up smoking but never seem to get around to it. We can even procrastinate when it comes to relationships. Perhaps you've decided that you want to look for a partner and start dating, for example, but never seem to find the time to join new groups or put up a profile on a dating website.

WHAT ARE THE DANGERS OF PROCRASTINATION?

Procrastination also carries health risks. For example, research shows that procrastinators are more likely to get sick. They also suffer higher levels of stress.[136]

Procrastination can also damage your relationships. If you delay making important decisions, such as when to buy a house or start a family, your partner's patience may run out. Procrastinate too much, and your loved one will eventually start questioning whether you really care about the relationship at all.

WHY DO WE DELAY TASKS?

We procrastinate because it offers some kind of pay-off. At first, this seems like a strange idea. Putting off important tasks leads to stress in the end, so why would anyone choose to delay them?

Put simply, procrastination makes you feel better in the short term. Suppose you have to write a long, complicated report at work. It's going to take several days, and the topic is boring. It doesn't sound very appealing, does it? If you tell yourself that you'll do it later, you immediately lower your stress levels. This sends a signal to your brain: "If we delay a task, the tension and stress goes away."

This is why procrastination is best thought of as an unhealthy habit. We get into the habit of responding to a trigger (e.g. a project or essay) with a behavior (delaying the task) that rewards us in some way (a drop in stress levels).

Psychologists have found that low levels of mindfulness are linked to procrastination.[137] People who procrastinate struggle to regulate their behaviors and emotions. This means they find it hard to force themselves to start tasks that are boring or unpleasant. By contrast, mindful individuals are better-equipped to recognize and accept their emotions, even the unpleasant ones, and continue to engage with tasks anyway.

What does this mean for you? If you start using the techniques in this book in your everyday life, you'll be less likely to procrastinate. You'll be able to tolerate discomfort and negative emotions. Tough tasks will still stress you out, but you won't feel the need to delay them so often.

PROCRASTINATION & NEGATIVE SELF-TALK

Sometimes, we procrastinate not just because we don't want to do the task, but because we don't want to endure negative self-talk or self-criticism. If you are in the habit of putting yourself down, you probably speak unkindly to yourself whenever you're facing a challenging task. Therefore, it makes sense that you'd want to avoid doing something that will trigger your inner critic.

For example, let's say you need to paint your living room. Painting a room, particularly if it's large, takes time and effort. But let's also suppose that you have low self-confidence and an active inner critic and you believe that all your DIY projects will end in failure. Painting a large room whilst having to listen to a voice telling you that your efforts are all in vain won't be an enticing prospect under those circumstances.

If you are a chronic procrastinator, you need to figure out whether your self-talk is holding you back. By noticing the way you talk to yourself, you can learn to stop identifying with your critic's harsh words.

Mindfulness Exercise: Noticing Your Inner Critic

1. The next time you find yourself feeling discouraged in the face of a big task or project, take a moment to slow down and check in with yourself.
2. Notice the thoughts racing through your head. Are they negative, positive, or neutral?
3. If you notice a critical voice, what is it like? Is it quiet or loud, male or female, snide or outright aggressive?
4. Every time a new critical thought pops up, label it. Say, "Oh, a critical thought" or "There's a critical voice."
5. Notice that each thought passes. Even if another comes along to take its place, no thought stays around forever.
6. Acknowledge your critic, and then start the task anyway. Take it slow; how could you make some progress in the next five or ten minutes?

There's no need to fight back against the unkind voice in your head. The difference between people who get things done and those who are held back by their insecurities is that the former have learned to acknowledge and accept it.

FINDING PURPOSE AT WORK

Do you ever arrive at work, look at your to-do list, and start asking, "What's the point?" When you're caught up in the daily grind, it's easy to lose your sense of purpose. Over time, you might become demotivated, disengaged, and depressed. You may start to procrastinate. After all, why bother putting in the work if you don't believe in it?

Mindfulness Exercise: Why Are You At Work?

Asking yourself a few questions each morning reminds you why your job is important, renews your sense of purpose, and keeps you focused.

At the start of every working day, ask yourself the following:

"What is my role here?"
"How can I better serve others?"
"What do I need to do today?"
"What must I do first?"

You can adapt these questions to your circumstances if you are a stay at home parent, student, or retiree.

Even if your work is dull and seems unimportant, you can still find some meaning if you look hard enough.

For example, suppose you have a boring entry-level administrative job at a small office. You may not find it easy to see the broader purpose of your role, but look closer.

You may be able to gain some satisfaction from cheering up other workers in your office or reminding yourself that, without your efforts, the business would quickly descend into chaos because no one would be keeping up with the mail. See your efforts as part of a greater whole.

WHY YOU NEED TO STOP MULTITASKING

We all like to think that we've mastered the art of doing several tasks at once. For instance, lots of us check our email while eating lunch, carrying on a conversation with a co-worker, and planning what to have for dinner. During the working day, our attention flits back and forth between various projects, phone calls, and so on.

Perhaps you are reading this book while watching a TV show or catching up on your emails. If so, switching off your devices and giving the book your complete attention is a small act of mindfulness in itself. As you continue reading, put the book down if you need to take a moment to think about an idea or exercise. As you read, think about how you could apply these principles in your everyday life.

Multitasking can make you feel productive. Unfortunately, this is just an illusion. Research shows that multitasking lowers your productivity.[138] Contrary to popular opinion, women aren't better at juggling tasks than men; both sexes are much worse off when they try to split their attention in several directions. It's not just a matter of practice, either. People who multitask often are actually worse at it![139]

If you get into the habit of multitasking, you lose your ability to focus long enough to assimilate new information. In other words, multitasking slowly undermines your ability to learn. For example, you can't pick up new information if your attention is split between your phone, your email, and an online article.[140]

MINDFULNESS & MONOTASKING

When you make a commitment to complete tasks mindfully, you are forced to slow down and put them in order. Then, you work your way through them, one at a time.

If you find the idea of focusing on a single task at a time uncomfortable, notice your thoughts and feelings. Does monotasking make you feel lazy? Do you feel as though you aren't productive unless you are juggling (or trying to juggle) multiple tasks? Does your body feel tense? Tune in and see what's going on inside.

Still skeptical? Stop multitasking for a week, and see what impact it has on both your professional and personal life.

TECH, PRODUCTIVITY, & PROCRASTINATION

Like it or not, technology has become an inescapable part of our lives. Most people assume that it's normal and harmless to spend hours every day glued to a screen, but have you ever stopped to consider the real cost of your tech habits, especially when it comes to your productivity?

It takes only a few moments to get sucked into a rabbit hole. We click an interesting looking link, which takes us to another website, which encourages us to share content on social media, and so on. It never ends!

Even if you only spend a few minutes browsing a website, your brain will be overwhelmed by information. We haven't evolved to cope with the sheer quantity of data that gets pumped into our heads every day, and it's almost impossible to perform well at work if we are distracted by our phones and the internet.

FEAR OF MISSING OUT (FOMO), ENVY, & INSECURITY

Do you have the feeling that other people are having a much better time than you? Does it seem like everyone else has an easier, more glamorous, and exciting life? You may be experiencing FOMO, a modern condition usually triggered by technology.

Before the rise of the internet, we didn't really have the chance to see what anyone outside our immediate social circle was doing. Now, it's all too easy to keep tabs on them and make comparisons.

If you have FOMO, you probably feel inferior to people on social media. You might feel envious of their jobs, relationships, or possessions. Poring over everyone's posts and photos won't make you feel great about yourself, and it can become a habit.

At worst, FOMO can be lethal. Some people are so worried that they'll miss some key update or post on their social media feed that they can't put their phones down when driving. Others waste so much time comparing themselves to everyone else that they become clinically depressed or anxious.

If you suffer from FOMO, you aren't living in the present. Your real problem isn't that you don't have someone else's "perfect" life. The real problem is that you are missing out on your own.

How To Use Tech Mindfully

So, is technology evil? Not at all! It's great for helping us keep in touch with people who matter to us, and it makes work a lot easier. Even if you wanted to, it would be almost impossible to escape it. We just have to figure out how to use technology in a mindful way.

Follow these tips for a healthier relationship with your devices:

Turn off all unnecessary notifications: Notifications interrupt your workflow, so turn them off. If you are worried about missing an interesting notification, acknowledge what's going on in your body and mind. Maybe your muscles feel tense, or perhaps you are experiencing a vague, low-level panic. Notice how it feels to go several hours without using your phone.

Use a tracker to monitor your use: We usually know when we're spending too much time online, but seeing raw data takes your awareness to a new level. There are lots of apps designed to help you lead a more mindful life. You may be in for a shock when you see the numbers!

Be mindful before reacting to people online: What do you do when you see or read something that makes you mad? Next time you start typing a response, pause for a moment and reflect on what you are trying to achieve. Be honest with yourself; what are your true motives?

Be aware that people seldom change their minds online and that fighting with someone usually ends in drama. Can you afford to let yourself be derailed by someone's Facebook or Twitter post?

The next time you are tempted to write an angry comment, notice what that urge feels like. See if you can surf it or wait it out instead of reacting. You'll feel calmer, you'll get more work done – and you won't get into so many pointless arguments.

Use mindfulness to overcome FOMO: Quitting social media is an effective cure for FOMO, but it isn't realistic for most people. If you have family and friends across the globe, there's no sense in cutting all virtual ties just because you've fallen into the habit of over-analyzing everyone else's lives.

So, what's the answer? Fortunately, research shows that being mindful reduces FOMO.[141] Staying aware of your emotions makes you less vulnerable to destructive envy. The next time you feel jealous, insecure, or sad when browsing social media, put your phone down for a moment and feel the emotion in your body. Feel it rise and fall. Breathe deeply. You'll notice that the emotion peaks within a few minutes.

Remind yourself that you have a choice. You are free to keep on browsing social media for hours at a time, but what's really going on? Are you simply addicted to making harmful comparisons, using the internet, or both?

Don't feed someone else's FOMO: When a social media post triggers your FOMO, maybe your first instinct is to post something that impresses your followers.

But take a moment to think about this a little more mindfully. When you participate in internet one-upmanship, be mindful of how your actions affect others. If you want to share photos and stories, do it with a sense of appreciation, gratitude, and joy.

SUMMARY

- Mindful people tend to procrastinate less often.
- We procrastinate when we feel overwhelmed by negative emotions or want to escape our inner critic.
- Mindfully accepting these thoughts and feelings makes tasks more tolerable, thus reducing procrastination.
- Mindful questions can help you locate a sense of purpose.
- Technology is an inescapable part of our lives, and we need to learn to use it mindfully.

CHAPTER 10:

BEATING "WHEN... THEN" SYNDROME WITH MINDFULNESS

So far, you've experimented with lots of mindfulness practices for specific problems like stress and depression. In this chapter, we're going to take a step back and look at the bigger picture. Mindfulness isn't just a useful approach for handling emotions on a day-to-day basis; it is a way of living.

ARE YOU LIVING FOR THE PRESENT OR THE FUTURE?

Do you tell yourself any of the following?

"When I land that new job, then I'll be happy."

"When I finally buy a new home, then I'll be happy."

"When I earn that promotion, then I can relax."

"When I find a partner, then I'll feel better about myself."

"When I lose 30lbs, then I'll feel better about my body."

These are examples of "When…Then" Syndrome in action. The main symptom is an obsession with making as much progress as you can, in the shortest possible amount of time, whilst ignoring what's going on around you.

If you're suffering from this affliction, you'll never be able to accept your life in the present moment. Instead, you'll pour all efforts into chasing whatever you think will make you happy. This is a tragedy because you will deprive yourself of the joys that come with living in the here and now.

Lots of people live like this. In fact, it's normal. If you were to ask your family and friends whether they are happy with their lives, they would probably tell you that they will be a lot happier when they finally manage to make some kind of major change.

WHY WE NEED TO ENJOY THE JOURNEY

Lots of us assume that we need to wait until we "arrive" at our destination before we feel happy. This perspective leads to nothing but pain. Why?

First, when you pin all your hopes for happiness on a single event or possession, you are vulnerable to disappointment. Few things live up to our expectations. That's just how life works. It's impossible to foresee every eventuality.

To make matters worse, human beings have a special ability to assume, often on an unconscious level, that success in one aspect of their lives will somehow change everything for the better. For example, you might trick yourself into thinking that a new relationship will somehow make you happy and that you will suddenly be able to launch yourself into a new career or finally commit to a diet.

Imagine that you drop dead tomorrow having never achieved your goals. It's a grim thought, isn't it? However, wouldn't it be even worse to die having never experienced life in the present because you were too busy striving towards a distant goal? The brutal truth is that you don't know whether the future will ever arrive. Doesn't it make more sense to focus on learning to live in the here and now?

Finally, by fixating on what you want, you are devaluing what you already have. For example, let's say you are working to get a promotion so that you can buy a bigger house. If you aren't careful, you'll start to slip into a dissatisfied state of mind. You may start feeling resentful that your boss doesn't pay you enough money, or that your current house isn't big enough. These thoughts keep you from slowing down and enjoying your life as it is right now. Given that it's the only life you have, you might as well savor it!

MINDFULNESS EXERCISE: HOW MUCH TIME DO YOU SPEND IN THE FUTURE?

Today, keep a piece of paper and a pen or pencil on hand. Every time you drift off into a daydream about the future, place a mark on the sheet of paper. At the end of the day, count them up. Are you surprised by how much time you spend time traveling?

CRAVINGS NEVER END

There is always something new to desire. We set a goal, work towards it, feel happy for a brief time when we meet it – then we start hankering after something new.

Until you realize that material possessions and status will never bring you true contentment, you are trapped in an uncomfortable cycle of striving, achieving, disappointment, more striving, etc. The only way to break free is to learn to live in the present.

Consider this: All your life, you have assumed that a particular person, possession, or title will make you happy. You already know that life doesn't work like that, or you wouldn't still be searching for contentment. Based on your experience so far, why would you think that your next achievement will be the one that really does make you happy?

When you accept that you will always want the next big thing, you are free to choose goals that are actually meaningful to you, and then to pursue them with an attitude of joy and curiosity rather than grim determination.

This isn't easy. We live in a materialistic world dominated by marketing campaigns that tell us the only true path to happiness is achievement and consumption. It takes courage to re-examine your values and go against the grain.

THE HEDONIC TREADMILL

If you are hoping that the "right" car, house, or widescreen TV will finally bring you contentment, you are headed for disappointment. Research has shown that accumulating memories, not material possessions, makes us happier.[142]

There's no doubt that buying gadgets or a new house can make you happy for a while, but we soon become desensitized to new luxuries. The elation wears off, and we start to look ahead to the next thing. This is known as hedonic adaptation, or the hedonic treadmill.

On the other hand, memories last forever, as do the feelings associated with them. If you mindfully enjoy the good times, you can conjure up these memories later and savor them all over again. Sharing experiences with others also strengthens your relationships, which in turn boosts your overall wellbeing and quality of life.

Think twice before investing in a fancy gadget you don't need. If you have some spare cash, why not put it towards an experience or adventure instead, preferably with people you love?

KEEP YOUR MIND & HEART OPEN

Life isn't predictable. The best-laid plans go awry. The good news is that you have a choice. You can try to keep up the illusion of control, or you can remain open to the idea of multiple possibilities. Think back over your life so far. Have there been times where everything went wrong, yet it worked out well in the end?

For example, you might have been fired from your job, but then found a much better position elsewhere. Or maybe the person you hoped to marry didn't feel the same way, but you later met someone who proved a more suitable match?

Maybe things won't work out as you'd like, but that doesn't mean you can't turn the situation to your advantage. At the very least, you can use disasters and setbacks as your teachers. Tough times are the perfect opportunity to practice your mindfulness skills.

You can feel happy anytime, anywhere, if you fully accept the present moment and engage in the dance of life.

SUMMARY

- Fixating on a future that may or may not arrive means you can't enjoy the present moment.
- Falling short of your goals isn't the worst thing that could happen to you; missing out on your life as it is right now is a greater tragedy.

- Don't make the mistake of assuming that an achievement in one area of your life will magically fix everything else.
- Material possessions make us happy but hedonic adaptation means that these pleasures don't last.
- Be open to what the future may bring, and don't hold too tightly to your expectations.

CHAPTER 11:

STAYING PRESENT WHILE PLANNING THE FUTURE

A t this point, you might be thinking along these lines: "Sure, staying in the present helps me live a more joyful life. But I can't stay in the present moment all the time! I've got to think about my future. I've got to make some plans!"

In this chapter, we'll look at how you can strike this delicate balance. You'll learn how to set mindful goals and make positive decisions.

MEDITATION & MINDFULNESS IN THE REAL WORLD

Most of us don't want to sell our houses, give away all our possessions, and move to a remote cave or monastery. We need mindfulness practices that work for ordinary people who lead ordinary lives.

Coach Brad Waters addresses this issue head-on in an article published in *Psychology Today*.[143] He notes that being mindful doesn't mean you have to float along in life without a plan. It means that when you do make plans, they come from a place of appreciation and acceptance of what you currently have. In fact, mindfulness is a great tool for setting goals.

Waters advises that mindful planning involves taking a close look at what you want to be, not just what you want to have. Asking questions like, "What is my place in the world?" and "What kind of relationships do I want to cultivate?" require more self-reflection than listing things you want to buy or the size of home you'd like to have.

The following exercise will help steer you in the right direction.

Mindfulness Exercise: Mindful Goal-Setting

The next time you set a goal, ask yourself the following questions:

1. Does this goal support my higher values?

    When your goals support your beliefs and wider vision, you are much more likely to stick with them. Working towards a value-driven goal will also be more satisfying. For instance, setting a weight loss goal because you value health makes sense. However, setting goals just for the sake of impressing others probably won't offer much intrinsic satisfaction.

2. Am I being realistic?

    Set goals that stretch you, not goals that leave you feeling overwhelmed before you even begin. Be honest with yourself. Remember that goals need to be right for you, not someone else or an imaginary version of yourself.

3. How will chasing this goal affect other people in my life? You probably don't live in a vacuum, and your goals could have a direct effect on your family, friends, and colleagues. You don't have to design your life around other people, but it's sensible to think mindfully about

the broader effects of your goals. You may need to adjust your goals slightly, or tweak your plans.

4. When I imagine achieving this goal, how does my body feel?

    Close your eyes and visualize the moment you achieve your goal. Tune into your body. How do you feel? Perhaps your heart rate has increased? Maybe you feel a rush of energy flowing through your body? Or do you find yourself sitting up straighter, in a more confident pose? These are all good signs that your goal is a great fit.

5. Am I willing to sit with the discomfort that will come with pursuing this goal?

    Chasing a meaningful goal will sometimes make you anxious. This is perfectly normal. As you now know, mindfulness practices will help you weather these emotions, accept them, and move forward. However, you need to be prepared to embrace your feelings, whatever they may be, at all stages of the journey.

6. Can I hold this goal lightly?

    As we saw in Chapter 10, clinging to a set of expectations is a recipe for disaster. Can you accept that you need to hold your goal lightly? Do you accept that your circumstances may change? As you'll see in the next section, it's good to take a flexible approach.

WHEN YOU START LIVING MINDFULLY, YOUR GOALS MIGHT CHANGE

Living moment to moment and finding peace and joy in everyday activities may change you on a profound level. Too many of us mindlessly go along with the goals society has set for us. We are told that wealth, good looks, status, and fame will make us happy. We are told to go to college, work hard, get a high-powered job, and buy as many toys and status symbols as possible.

However, when you make mindfulness a part of your life, you'll probably start questioning these values. For example, you might decide that time spent in mindful relaxation with your family is more valuable than working long hours to land your next big promotion. Your old goals may no longer fit your personal aims and values. It's OK to change your goals. Review them whenever your intuition tells you it's time.

Mindfulness Improves Decision-Making

Have you ever felt torn between two or more options? Are you overwhelmed whenever you need to make a big decision? Great news: mindfulness can help you out.

Not only can mindfulness be successfully combined with decision-making, but it can improve your ability to make sensible choices.

Mindfulness Exercise: Decision-Making

Here's how to make a mindful choice:[144]

1. Be aware that you need to make the best possible decision, not a perfect decision. Acknowledge that you are in a state of confusion. Take a few deep breaths. Reassure yourself that you can only do your best with the information and resources you have available to you right now.

2. Tune into your goals and values. When decision-making is tough, it's often because two or more of your values are colliding.

   For instance, suppose you have to choose whether to walk away from your job at a small, family-run firm. On one hand, you may value loyalty and stability, which makes you reluctant to leave. At the same time, you might also value creative expression and ambition, which makes you want to seek a different kind of work.

   The best decisions support as many of your values as possible, but sometimes there seems to be no winning. Reframe the situation as a chance to learn and grow. You may have to acknowledge that one of your values has to take on greater importance relative to others.

3. Weigh each option carefully. Notice whether you tend to place more weight on emotional factors than intellectual factors, or vice versa. Mindfully encourage yourself to address the problem from both sides.

4. Ask, "What might I be missing here?" and "Is there anything I'm forgetting about?" Be patient with yourself.

   You'll notice a degree of discomfort when you have to make a decision, and it's this feeling that means we tend to delay them as long as possible. When we make a choice, we're giving up a sense of control. When we rule out one or more options, we are limiting our opportunities.

We often worry about making the wrong decision. We get carried away, dreaming up all kinds of scenarios in which we come to regret our choices. Mindfulness helps you accept this discomfort, which empowers you to make more decisions in the future. You'll learn to trust yourself and how to accept the outcome of your choices.

Summary

- You can learn how to balance mindfulness with long-term planning and decision-making.
- Mindful goals align with our deepest values.
- Leading a more mindful life often prompts us to re-evaluate our goals.
- Mindful decision-making entails taking a realistic look at all our options, weighing up the practical and emotional dimensions of each, and making the best decision based on the resources we have.

CHAPTER 12:

MINDFULNESS & RELATIONSHIPS

Relationships can be hard work. The good news is that adopting a more mindful way of life can strengthen your relationships, help you resolve arguments, and generally feel happier around other people.

In this chapter, we'll focus on romantic relationships, but the principles and exercises apply to friendships, family relationships, and even work relationships.

What Does A Mindful Relationship Look Like?

At the beginning of your relationship, you were probably mindful of one another. You were on your best behavior. You tried to impress them with your kindness, humor, and devotion. Your priority was to keep them happy, hoping that they would stick around. When you were apart, you probably thought about them all the time.

Unfortunately, once we've settled into a relationship, we often start taking our partners for granted. Other concerns, such as work or starting a family, start to take up more of our attention.

No honeymoon period lasts forever, but you can keep your relationship intimate and fresh by making a commitment to loving your partner in a mindful way. So, what does this mean? A mindful relationship looks like this:

- Both parties feel respected.
- Both parties feel as though their partner truly listens to them.
- Both parties know that their partner is interested in them as a person.
- Both parties know that their partner finds them attractive.
- Disagreements are handled sensitively but directly.
- Both parties understand that relationships require ongoing maintenance if they are to succeed.

Sounds good, doesn't it? Mindful relationships aren't perfect, but they are far more satisfying than sliding into the kind of rut that many of us know all too well.

COMMUNICATION: THE KEY TO SUCCESSFUL RELATIONSHIPS

Poor communication causes resentment and misunderstandings, which can ultimately ruin a relationship. All too often, we don't bother to check that we've understood what someone else is saying. Or, even worse, we don't listen properly in the first place.

For instance, are you guilty of using your phone or reading a magazine when a partner or friend is trying to talk to you? If so, you're putting your relationship in jeopardy. Your loved one probably feels disrespected and resentful, which isn't a good basis for love or friendship.

HOW TO BE A GREAT LISTENER

When was the last time you spoke to someone who really listened to what you had to say? Someone who gave you their full attention, listened mindfully, and never interrupted? These folks are rare – and popular! They tend to have lots of friends, and they enjoy satisfying relationships. Imagine how much better your own relationships will be when you start interacting mindfully with others.

Mindfulness Exercise: Mindful Listening

1. When someone tries to start a conversation, you need to make a decision: Can you give them the attention they need and deserve, or would it be better to delay the conversation? If it's the latter, ask if you can talk later. Explain that you want to really listen to what they have to say, and you'd rather not multitask.

2. When it's time to have the conversation, stop whatever you're doing and pay attention.

3. Maintain eye contact.

4. Try not to think about what you're going to say next. Wait until the other person has finished speaking before thinking of a response. Often, we fall into the trap of becoming distracted by our own thoughts or judgments. This prevents us from appreciating what someone is trying to tell us.

5. Hold back when it comes to giving advice. If someone asks for your opinion, then give it, but be aware that they might just want a chance to vent.

6. Try to maintain an attitude of compassionate curiosity. Until you have evidence to the contrary, assume that the other person is acting with positive intent.

Listening is a key skill for mindful arguing. As you know, mindfulness helps develop impulse control and patience, which could make all the difference to the outcome of a fight.

During tense conversations, pause – if only for two or three seconds – before responding to a provocative statement or question. Be kind to yourself. Acknowledge that you are in a tough spot and recognize any anxiety or anger that comes up. Rehearse answers in your head before speaking aloud. It's far better to take your time than say something you'll later regret. If you feel overwhelmed, excuse yourself for a couple of minutes to think through your options.

Judgments

Do you judge others? You're in good company. Almost everyone does it; it's just human nature. We also tend to jump to conclusions about someone else's behavior, even when we don't have much evidence to support our beliefs.

For example, you may notice that your partner has left some crumbs on the kitchen table, and you automatically say to yourself, "They're so messy and lazy." Or maybe they have been late home twice this week so you jump to the conclusion that they must be having an affair or that they want to avoid spending time with you.

When we start passing judgment on everyone else's behaviors, we get into trouble. We get so caught up in reacting to what they've said or done – or what we think they've done or said – that we start acting irrationally.

We don't have to get swept up in our judgments. Instead, we can choose to be mindful when they pop up. No matter how compelling your emotions, try not to assume that they are a true reflection of reality. When you find yourself angry or upset at someone else, take a few deep breaths and pay attention to what you are actually thinking and feeling. Notice each judgment. Imagine it as a bubble floating away on a breeze, or as a leaf in a stream flowing past you.

This takes practice. Judging others, whether or not we admit it, can feel good. Self-righteousness can give us a kind of energy, and even boost our self-esteem. You'll never get rid of your impulse to judge people, but you can definitely use mindfulness to limit its effect on your relationships.

ARE YOU HOPING THAT SOMEONE ELSE WILL CHANGE?

If you've been embarking on a period of personal growth, you've probably felt frustrated and baffled by your own behavior. Mindfulness will help you grow as a person and get more enjoyment out of life, but it isn't easy. It takes time to learn new skills, and mindfulness is no exception.

Given that we have enough trouble understanding and changing ourselves, it's foolish to expect someone else to change on demand. Everyone evolves on their own schedule, and some people never seem to grow much, if at all. To put it bluntly, someone else's path is none of your business, even if that "someone" happens to be your partner or relative.

So, if you think you'll be happy when your partner becomes more patient, or your parents become more understanding, it's time to adjust your expectations. Stop wasting your precious time and energy. Work on accepting them as they are. Your relationships will improve because you won't feel so resentful. You'll also feel free to walk away from relationships that hold you back.

Loving-Kindness Meditation, which involves sending warmth and love to someone else, helps you accept and appreciate others. Refer back to Chapter Three if you need a refresher. Practice for a few minutes every day when your relationship is going through a rough patch.

It also helps to see the other person as a teacher. When someone can't (or won't) live up to your expectations, they are teaching you a valuable lesson about accepting life as it is, not as you want it to be. When you decide to honor who someone truly is, you'll both feel better!

Paradoxically, when you decide to show someone compassion and acceptance, they are more likely to change. If you've been practicing mindfulness, you'll already have seen this phenomenon in your own life. You've probably noticed that since you started coming face to face with your thoughts and emotions and detaching yourself from self-judgment, your life is starting to take a more positive course.

MINDFULNESS DOESN'T MAKE YOU A HUMAN DOORMAT

Mindfulness helps us accept other people's annoying behaviors and makes it easier to show them compassion. You may worry that you'll end up going too far and making too many allowances for poor or abusive behavior.

However, being mindful isn't the same as being a pushover or doormat. In fact, mindfulness helps you assert your rights and pick up on signs of abuse quickly.

When you are in tune with your emotions and don't try to write them off or make excuses for others, you'll find it easier to maintain a realistic view of your relationships. Staying in the present moment lets you monitor events as they unfold. You can take a more objective stance, and decide exactly how the other person is making you feel. You will choose partners and friends on the basis of who they really are, not who you want them to be.

SUMMARY

- A mindful relationship is built on trust, respect, and a realistic view of the other person's strengths and weaknesses.
- Mindful communication, including mindful listening, will strengthen any partnership.
- Arguments are inevitable, but approaching them mindfully makes a big difference.
- Your relationship will improve if you accept your partner for who they are and release unrealistic ideas of who you want them to be.

CHAPTER 13:

MAKING MINDFULNESS PART OF EVERYDAY LIFE

Modern life is hectic, so how can the average person make time for mindfulness practices? In this chapter, we'll take a look at how you can weave mindfulness into your everyday routine.

WHAT DOES A MINDFUL DAY LOOK LIKE?

Don't try to do everything on this list because you'll soon get overwhelmed. Instead, pick one or two of the habits listed below and try to do them consistently for at least three weeks. You can then add another daily practice if you like. There is no single path to mindfulness; you need to find what works best for you.

MINDFUL MORNINGS

1. Greet the day with mindfulness.
    When you open your eyes, resist the urge to reach for your phone. Instead, take a minute to notice how you feel. What expectations do you have for the day ahead?

Do you feel tired or well-rested? Having acknowledged your feelings, slowly get out of bed. If you don't want to get up, try not to argue with yourself – just focus on the sensation of moving your body.

2. Make your bed.
   Making your bed is a good morning ritual. It's an easy task that sets you up for the day. Plus, it's always nicer to climb into a well-made bed in the evening.

3. Have a mindful drink of water.
   Pay attention to the feel of the glass in your hand. Notice any water droplets or condensation and whether the glass catches the light coming in through the window. As you drink the water, feel it moving from your mouth to your stomach.

4. Greet your partner, pets, roommates, or children in a kind and mindful manner.
   Do you snap or grunt at others in the morning? Try greeting them as though you may never see them again. Take a moment to feel grateful that they are in your life.

DURING THE DAY

1. Spend time in a natural setting.
   Ten minutes in a park or garden will restore your mental equilibrium, which in turn will make you more mindful. If you can't get outside, at least stand or sit by the window for a few minutes.

2. Give yourself a mindful smile.
   How often do you take a moment to appreciate what you see in the mirror? Lots of us look at our reflections

when we shave or put on makeup, but we don't often slow down and take a moment to appreciate ourselves. If we do slow down long enough to take a good look, our inner critic usually kicks in, telling us that we are too fat, too ugly, too old, and so forth. If you need to ground yourself, find a quiet place and look at your own face in a mirror. Look at it as though for the first time, taking in the colors, lines, and contours. If any harsh thoughts come up, label them as such and let them go. When you're ready, give yourself a smile. Feel the love and light radiate from your face.

3. Let yourself laugh.

Laughing is a form of mindfulness. When you laugh, you are grounded in the present. Find a few funny video clips to enjoy, reflect on a fond memory, or share a joke with someone else.

4. Eat and drink mindfully.

You might not be able to do this with every meal or snack, but try to have at least one mindful meal per day. Refer back to Chapter Two for more tips on how to eat mindfully. When you make a cup of tea or coffee, pay attention to the process. Notice the water bubbling as it reaches boiling point. Notice the color of your drink, the steam, and how the cup or mug feels in your hands. Savor the taste.

5. Use tech mindfully

Refer back to Chapter Nine for tips on how to unchain yourself from your devices.

6. Use mindfulness practices to overcome procrastination. Chapter Nine contains lots of useful exercises that will help you remain calm in the face of a long to-do list.

7. Embrace waiting as a chance to practice.
Next time you are stuck in traffic or waiting in a long line, use the time to put away your phone, take a few deep breaths, and notice what is going on around you. Acknowledge that you are frustrated or bored, and the waiting will probably seem more bearable.

EASING THE TRANSITION FROM WORK TO HOME

1. End your day on a mindful note
Before you leave work, congratulate yourself for completing your tasks. Even if your colleagues or boss don't appreciate your efforts, you can give yourself some well-earned praise. Show yourself some appreciation.

2. Use a mindfulness ritual to help you switch off from work
Develop a mindfulness practice that you use only at the end of the day. For example, if you work in an office, you could make a habit of slowly walking down the hallway when you leave, feeling your feet against the floor.

3. Be a mindful commuter
Commuting is a perfect opportunity to practice mindfulness. Pay attention to the temperature of your car, train, or bus, the view from your window, and how it feels to sit in your seat. If you use public transportation or walk to and from work, why not listen to a guided meditation?

MINDFULNESS IN THE EVENING

1. Carry out your chores mindfully

   Washing the dishes, cleaning the bathroom, doing the laundry – most chores are a wonderful opportunity to practice using your senses in a mindful way. For example, if you are doing the laundry, focus on how the fabric feels against your skin, the scent of the detergent when you remove it from the machine, or the gentle noise of the tumble dryer. As you fold the clothes, take a moment to appreciate the fact you have garments to keep you warm (or cool, depending on your climate!), and that you have the equipment to keep them clean.

2. Take a mindful shower

   As you step into the shower, notice how the air feels against your skin. Is it cool or warm? Turn on the shower and let the water hit your skin. Adjust the temperature up and down. Turn around slowly and notice how the water feels against different parts of your body. Are some parts more sensitive than others?

   When you squeeze shower gel or shampoo from the bottle, notice its texture, temperature, and scent. Is it strong or subtle? Fresh or musky? Does it foam? If you use a loofah or sponge, rub it gently against your skin for a minute, then use firmer strokes. Notice the change in sensation.

3. Review your day

   Just before you go to bed, look back over your day and think about when you were most mindful. Review the mindfulness practices you used. Which worked best for you? If you didn't manage to be mindful, that's OK. No one is perfect, and you can always try again tomorrow.

4. Practice gratitude before you go to sleep
   Give thanks for all the good things that happened to you during the day. Even if everything seemed to go wrong, you can still be grateful for the basics. Never take things like access to clean water, shelter, and food for granted. Some people prefer to practice gratitude in the morning to set them up for the day ahead.

BE PREPARED

You've probably heard the saying, "Fail to prepare, and you prepare to fail." This applies when working with habits. Take a moment to think about the barriers you might face. For instance, let's say you want to start every day with a five-minute gratitude practice.

Perhaps you're worried about drifting off to sleep and being late for work as a result. Or maybe you just have a feeling that you won't feel like spending time practicing mindfulness in the morning and would prefer to jump straight in the shower instead as usual.

With a little initiative, both of these barriers can be overcome. For example, you could make it a habit to sit up on the edge of your bed as soon as you wake up or decide to do your gratitude practice in the shower instead. You could write a note to yourself and keep it on your bedside table to read on those mornings when the last thing you want to do is set aside five minutes to be mindful.

Get An Accountability Buddy

Do you know someone else who is interested in mindfulness and personal development? If so, why not suggest you support one another on your mindfulness journeys? Checking in with a quick phone call or text message a few times per week can keep you both on track. If you don't know anyone who might be suitable, look for a buddy online. There are lots of communities, such as freemindfulness.org, where you can meet like-minded people.

Taking Your Practice Further

If you have time, set aside longer periods – say 20 to 30 minutes per day – for an extended period of practice. You could get up earlier in the morning or start your bedtime routine a half hour earlier than usual. You could even find a quiet room during your lunch break at work to meditate or engage in another mindful practice.

When you make an appointment with yourself, honor it, just as you would a meeting with a friend or coworker. If you feel a sense of resistance to scheduling time for yourself, take a moment and think about why this might be. Can you feel the resistance in your body? Does the thought of taking time for yourself feel somehow "wrong" or selfish?

If so, gently remind yourself of the benefits of mindfulness. Take an attitude of self-compassion. Caring for yourself, especially in a world that demands we put others' needs before our own, can be scary. Yet prioritizing your wellbeing can actually help those around you. For example, if you are a parent, living a more mindful life will help you remain calm when your kids are testing your patience. Your children are also more likely to develop emotional intelligence if they have parents who model healthy behaviors.

SUMMARY

- To get the most from mindfulness practice, you need to make it a part of your everyday life.
- You can practice mindfulness at any time of day. Mundane tasks and chores often provide the perfect opportunity to engage all your senses and ground yourself in the present moment.
- Anticipate barriers to your practice and think of ways around them.
- An accountability buddy will help keep you on track.
- If you have time, aim for 20-30 minutes of practice per day.
- You are only human. Don't worry if you fall back into old habits occasionally.

CONCLUSION

Congratulations! You've discovered how to live in the present. The daily grind is no longer quite so joyless now that you can find contentment in every moment. Your relationships will blossom as others feel drawn to your positive energy. You'll find new meaning in your career, hobbies, and friendships.

The more time you make for your mindfulness practices, the lighter and freer you will become. When you feel yourself slipping into mindless behavior, you will pull yourself back to reality within seconds.

Your family, friends, and colleagues will soon notice the shift in your outlook. You'll get compliments like:

"You seem so content lately."
"You're looking so relaxed!"
"Wow, I wish I could be as calm as you."

They will start asking for your "secret." Point them in the direction of this book and encourage them to experience the power of mindfulness for themselves. Offer to share a few of your favorite practices. Why not suggest a mindful walk or meal together?

Mindfulness has the power to heal the world. If we all took time to notice and accept our emotions instead of acting on impulse and then judging ourselves, imagine how things would change. Everyone would be kinder. Relationships would be easier. Old grudges would be forgotten.

Society is gradually waking up. More than ever, we need to live consciously, accept our differences, and join together to shape our collective future. You are now part of this movement. Isn't that exciting?

You may only be one person, but your actions have a ripple effect. Treating yourself and others with quiet appreciation and respect softens your attitude to life. You will start seeing opportunity and blessings wherever you look. Sure, you'll come up against challenges, but you can handle them.

From now on, your mindfulness practice is your refuge, open at all hours of the day and night. Whatever happens, you'll always be able to surf even the biggest of waves. Embrace change, show compassion to yourself and others, and treasure this moment. Ultimately, it's all any of us have.

THANKS FOR READING!

I really hope you enjoyed this book, and most of all – got more value from it than you had to give.

It would mean a lot to me if you left an Amazon review – I will reply to all questions asked!

Simply find this book on Amazon, scroll to the reviews section, and click "Write a customer review". Or alternatively please visit www.pristinepublish.com/cbtbundlereview to leave a review.

Be sure to check out my email list, where I am constantly adding tons of value.

The best way to get on the list currently is by visiting www.pristinepublish.com/meditationbonus and entering your email.

Here I'll provide actionable information that aims to improve your enjoyment of life.

I'll update you on my latest books and I'll even send free e-books that I think you'll find useful.

Kindest regards,

Olivia Telford

Also by
Olivia Telford

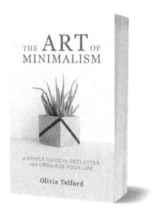

With Hygge and Minimalism you will discover something that offers relaxation, happiness, and contentment, all rolled into one. They encompass the positivity and enjoyment that one can get from simple everyday things.

Visit: www.pristinepublish.com/olivia

REFERENCES

[1] Hofmann, S.G., Asnaani, A., Vonk, I.J.J., Sawyer, A.T., & Fang, A. The Efficacy of Cognitive Behavioral Therapy: A Review of Meta-analyses. *Cognitive Therapy Research.*

[2] Jazaieri, H., Goldin, P.R., & Gross, J.J. (2017). Treating Social Anxiety Disorder with CBT: Impact on Emotional Regulation and Satisfaction with Life. *Cognitive Therapy Research.*

[3] Geukes, K., van Zalk, M., & Back, M.D. (2018). Understanding personality development: An integrative state process model. International Journal of Behavioral Development.

[4] Fenn, K., & Byrne, M. (2013). The key principles of cognitive behavioural therapy. *InnovAiT: Education and inspiration for general practice.*

[5] McLeod, S. (2019). *Cognitive Behavioural Therapy.*

[6] Martin, B. (2019). *In-Depth: Cognitive Behavioral Therapy.*

[7] McLeod, S.A. (2019). *Cognitive Behavioral Therapy.*

[8] Selva, J. (2018). *Albert Ellis' ABC Model in the Cognitive Behavioral Therapy Spotlight.*

[9] David, D. (n.d.). *Rational Emotive Behavior Therapy in the Context of Modern Psychological Research.*

[10] Cherry, K. (2019). *Psychologist Aaron Beck Biography.*

[11] Linehan, M.M. (2015). *DBT Skills Training Manual*. NY, New York: Guilford Press.

[12] Hayes, S.C., Luoma, J.B., Bond, F.W., Masuda, A., & Lillis, J. (2006). Acceptance and Commitment Therapy: Model, processes, and outcomes. *Psychology Faculty Publications*.

[13] Williams, M. (n.d.). *MBCT.*

[14] Warrilow, A.E., & Beech, B. (2009). Self-help CBT for depression: Opportunities for primary care mental health nurses? *Journal of Psychiatric Mental Health Nursing.*

[15] Morin, A. (2019). *Depression Statistics Everyone Should Know.*

[16] Burcusa, S.L., & Iacono, W.G. (2007). Risk for recurrence in depression. *Clinical Psychology Review.*

[17] NICE. (2018). *Appendix: Assessing depression and its severity.*

[18] Carter, C.L. (2017). Depression, Antidepressants and Cognitions: Silent Schemas in the Walking Wounded. *Journal of Psychology and Psychotherapy.*

[19] Kovacs, M., & Beck, A.T. (1978). Maladaptive Cognitive Structures in Depression. *American Journal of Psychiatry.*

[20] Rnic, K., Dozois, D.J.A., Martin, R.A. (2016). Cognitive Distortions, Humor Styles, and Depression. *European Journal of Psychology.*

[21] Concordia University. (n.d.). *Examples of Cognitive Restructuring.*

[22] National Institute for Health Research. (n.d.). *Behavioural activation – a simple therapy for depression.*

[23] Tull, M. (2019). *8 Tips for Using Behavioral Activation to Treat Depression.*

[24] Bell, A.C., & D'Zurilla, T.J. (2009). Problem-solving therapy for depression: A meta-analysis. *Clinical Psychology Review.*

[25] UC Davis. (n.d.). *Understanding Insomnia.*

[26] Harvard Health Publishing. (2009). *Insomnia: Restoring restful sleep.*

[27] WebMD. (n.d.). *Understanding Sleep Problems – The Basics.*

[28] Kyle, S. (n.d.). *What is Insomnia?*

[29] UC Davis. (n.d.). *Sleep Scheduling and Stimulus Control Techniques.*

[30] National Sleep Foundation. (n.d.). *The Ideal Temperature for Sleep.*

[31] UC Davis. (n.d.). *Cognitive Restructuring.*

[32] Anxiety UK. (n.d.) *What Is Anxiety?*

[33] NHS. (2018). *Do I have an anxiety disorder?*

[34] Centre for Clinical Interventions. (n.d.) *The vicious cycle of anxiety.*

[35] Kaplan, J.S., & Tolin, D.F. (2011). Exposure Therapy for Anxiety Disorders. *Psychiatry Times.*

[36] WebMD. (n.d.). *What if My Panic Attacks Won't Stop?*

[37] Anxiety Canada. (n.d.) *Self-Help Strategies For Panic Disorder.*

[38] Singer, J. (2018). *Interoceptive Exposures for Those with Panic Disorder.*

[39] Yonkers, K.A., Bruce, S.E., Dyck, I.R., & Keller, M.B. (2003). Chronicity, relapse, and illness-course of panic disorder, social phobia, and generalized anxiety disorder: findings in men and women from 8 years of follow-up. *Depression and Anxiety.*

[40] NHS. (2016). *Obsessive compulsive disorder (OCD).*

[41] Ibid.

[42] International OCD Foundation. (n.d.) *What Is OCD?*

[43] Anxiety Canada. (n.d.) *Vicious Cycle of OCD: How OCD Takes Over.*

[44] Singer, J. (2018). *OCD and the Need for Reassurance.*

[45] OCD-UK. (n.d.). *What is Exposure Response Prevention (ERP)?*

[46] Anxiety Canada. (n.d.). *Self-Help: Managing Your OCD At Home.*

[47] Tompkins, M.A. (2016). *Nuts and Bolts of Imaginal Exposure.*

[48] Rozental, A., & Carlbring, P. (2013). Internet-Based Cognitive Behavior Therapy for Procrastination: Study Protocol for a Randomized Controlled Trial. *JMIR Research Protocols.*

[49] Rozental, A., & Carlbring, P. (2014). Understanding and Treating Procrastination: A Review of a Common Self-Regulatory Failure. *Psychology.*

[50] Jaffe, E. (2013). *Why Wait? The Science Behind Procrastination.*

[51] Chard, P. (2018). *Fear, not laziness, is what fuels procrastination.*

[52] Burns, D.D. (2008). *Feeling Good: The New Mood Therapy.* New York, NY: Harper Collins.

[53] Loder, V. (2016). *10 Scientifically Proven Tips for Beating Procrastination.*

[54] Enright, R. (2018). *Conquering Your Regrets: Seven Suggestions for Self-Release.*

[55] Shannon, J. (n.d.). *Responsibility Pie.*

[56] Nevid, J.S. (2017). *Guilt Me Not.*

[57] Brenner, A. (2011). *5 Ways to Find Closure From the Past.*

[58] Mental Health America. (n.d.). *Rest, Relaxation, and Exercise.*

[59] NHS. (n.d.). *Addiction: What Is It?*

[60] Priory Group. (n.d.). *How to spot the signs of an addiction.*

[61] Legg, T.J. (2018). *What are the risk factors for addiction?*

[62] Treatnet. (n.d.). *Elements of Psychological Treatment.*

[63] McGee, M. (2017). *Managing External Triggers.*

[64] Newman, C. (2016). *Treating Substance Misuse Disorders with CBT.*

[65] Heshmat, S. (2015). *Why Cravings Occur.*

[66] Kassani, A., Niazi, M., Hassanzadeh, J., & Menati, R. (2015). Survival Analysis of Drug Abuse Relapse in Addiction Treatment Centers. *International Journal of High Risk Behaviors & Addiction.*

[67] Heshmat, S. (2015). *Why Cravings Occur.*

[68] Leahy, R.L., & Tirch, D.D. (2008). Cognitive Behavioral Therapy for Jealousy. *International Journal of Cognitive Therapy.*

[69] Ibid.

[70] Ibid.

[71] Firestone, L. (2011). *What Drives Jealousy?*

[72] Seltzer, L.F. (2009). *Why Criticism Is So Hard to Take (Part 1).*

[73] Mayo Clinic. (n.d.) *Being assertive: Reduce stress, communicate better.*

[74] Tartakovsky, M. (2018). *What So Many of Us Get Wrong About Assertiveness.*

[75] Collingwood, J. (2018). *Learning To Say No.*

[76] Michel, F., & Fursland, A. (2008). *How to Behave More Assertively.*

[77] Ibid.

[78] Greenberg, B. (2018). *8 Secrets to Handling Criticism Well.*

[79] Michel, F., & Fursland, A. (2008). *How to Deal Assertively with Criticism.*

[80] Kabat-Zinn, J. (2003). Mindfulness-Based Interventions in Context: Past, Present, and Future. *Clinical Psychology: Science and Practice.*

[81] Harley Therapy. (2014). *CBT vs MBCT – What is the Difference?*

[82] Oxford Mindfulness Centre. (2016). *MBCT for recurrent depression: What do we know? What does it mean? Where to next?*

[83] Schroevers, M.J., Tovote, K.A., Snippe, E., & Fleer, J. (2016). Group and Individual Mindfulness-Based Cognitive Therapy (MBCT) Are Both Effective: a Pilot Randomized Controlled Trial in Depressed People with a Somatic Disease. *Mindfulness.*

[84] Metzner, R. (1996). The Buddhist six-worlds model of consciousness and reality. *The Journal of Transpersonal Psychology.*

[85] Byron Clinic. (n.d.). *Marsha Linehan on Radical Acceptance.*

[86] Mindful Magazine. (2014). *What is Mindfulness?*

[87] Shapiro, S.L., Carlson, L.E., Astin, J.A., & Freedman, B. (2006). Mechanisms of Mindfulness. *Journal of Clinical Psychology.*

[88] Tricycle. (2017). *The Mindfulness of the Buddha.*

[89] Thera, S. (1998). *The Way of Mindfulness: The Satipatthana Sutta and Its Commentary.*

[90] O'Brien, B. (2017). *The Four Foundations of Mindfulness.*

[91] Center for Mindfulness. (n.d.). *MBSR: Mindfulness-Based Stress Reduction.*

[92] *Condon, P., Desbordes, G., Miller, W.B., & DeSteno, D. (2013). Meditation Increases Compassionate Responses to Suffering. Psychological Science.*

[93] de Vibe, M, et al. (2013). Mindfulness training for stress management: a randomised controlled study of medical and psychology students. BMC Medical Education.

[94] Wachs, K., & Cordova, J.V. (2007). Mindful Relating: Exploring Mindfulness & Emotion Repertoire in Intimate Relationships. *Journal of Marital and Family Therapy.*

[95] Zeidan, F., Johnson, S.K., Diamond, B.J., David, Z., & Goolkasian, P. (2010). Mindfulness meditation improves cognition: Evidence of brief mental training. *Consciousness and Cognition.*

[96] Black, D.S., & Slavich, G.M. (2016). Mindfulness meditation and the immune system: a systematic review of randomized control trials. *Annals of the New York Academy of Science.*

[97] The Tavistock & Portman NHS Foundation Trust. (n.d.). *Mindfulness: A self-help guide.*

[98] Smookler, E. (2016). *Beginner's Body Scan Meditation.*

[99] Brady, A. (n.d.). *Mindful Walking Practice: How to Get Started.*

[100] Thorpe, M. (2017). *12 Science-Based Benefits of Meditation.*

[101] Dienstmann, G. (n.d.). *Mantra Meditation – The Why, the How, and the Methods.*

[102] Koreyva, W. (n.d.). *Learn to Meditate in 6 Easy Steps.*

[103] Greater Good in Action. (n.d.). *Loving-Kindness Meditation.*

[104]<?> Science Daily. (2017). *Yoga, Meditation improve brain function and energy levels, study shows.*

[105] Konkel, L. (n.d.). *Cortisol: Everything You Need to Know About the "Stress Hormone."*

[106] Brand, S., Holsboer-Trachsler, E., Naranjo, J.R., & Schmidt, S. (2012). Influence of Mindfulness Practice on Cortisol and Sleep in Long-Term and Short-Term Meditators. *Neuropsychobiology.*

[107] Positive Psychology Program. (2017). *MBSR: 25 Mindfulness-Based Stress Reduction Exercises and Courses.*

[108] Luken, M., & Sammons, A. (2016). Systematic Review of Mindfulness Practice for Reducing Job Burnout. *American Journal of Occupational Therapy.*

[109] O'Brien, M. (n.d.). *How to Use Mindfulness to Work with Negative Emotions.*

[110] Abblett, M. (2017). *How Labels Help: Tame Reactive Emotions by Naming Them.*

[111] Buggy, P. (n.d.). *6 Mindful Strategies for Dealing with Negativity.*

[112] Domet, S. (2018). *A Simple Mindful Gratitude Exercise.*

[113] Van Oyen Witvliet, C., Richie, F.J., & Root Luna, L.M., & Van Tongeren, D.R. (2018). Gratitude predicts hope and happiness: A two-study assessment of traits and states. *The Journal of Positive Psychology.*

[114] Schutte, N.S., & Malouff, J.M. (2011). Emotional intelligence mediates the relationship between mindfulness and subjective well-being. *Personality and Individual Differences.*

[115] Ibid.

[116] Dansiger, S. (2016). *Mindfulness for Anger Management: Transformative Skills for Overcoming Anger and Managing Powerful Emotions.* Emeryville, CA: Althea Press.

[117] Dummies. (n.d.). *How to Use Mindfulness to Cope with Anger.*

[118] NHS. (n.d.). *Symptoms: Clinical Depression.*

[119] NHS. (2019). *Mindfulness.*

[120] Beck Institute for Cognitive Behavioral Therapy. (n.d.) *History of Cognitive Behavioral Therapy.*

[121] Morrison, A.B., Goolsarran, M., Rogers, S.L., & Jha, A.J. (2014). Taming a wandering attention: Short-form mindfulness training in student cohorts. *Frontiers in Human Neuroscience.*

[122] Positive Psychology Program. (2018). *Gratitude Meditation: A Simple*

but Powerful Happiness Intervention.

[123] Positive Psychology Program. (2017). *22 Mindfulness Exercises, Techniques & Activities for Adults.*

[124] Chiesa, A., & Serretti, A. (2011). Mindfulness based cognitive therapy for psychiatric disorders: A systematic review and meta-analysis. *Psychiatry Research.*

[125] Positive Psychology Program. (2019). *What is MBCT?*

[126] Hofmann, S.G., & Gomez, A.F. (2017). Mindfulness-Based Interventions for Anxiety and Depression. *Psychiatric Clinics of North America.*

[127] Abblett, M., & D'Antuono, J. (2016). *Why It's Difficult to Meditate with Anxiety.*

[128] Aryaloka Buddhist Center. (n.d.) *Mandalas as a spiritual practice.*

[129] Goldstein, E. (2013). *STOP.*

[130] National Institute for the Clinical Application of Behavioral Medicine. (n.d.). *A Simple Mindfulness Practice That Can Lower Anxiety.*

[131] Byrne, H. (2016). *The Here-and-New Habit: How Mindfulness Can Help You Break Unhealthy Habits Once and for All.* Oakland, CA: New Harbinger Publications.

[132] Kahneman, D. (2012). *Thinking, Fast and Slow.* London, England: Penguin Books Ltd.

[133] Brewer, J. (2017). *A Simple Way to Break a Bad Habit.*

[134] Clear, J. (n.d.). *How Long Does It Actually Take to Form A New Habit? (Backed By Science).*

[135] Portland Psychotherapy. (n.d). *Riding the Wave: Using Mindfulness to Help Cope with Urges.*

[136] Tice, D.M., & Baumeister, R.F. (1997). Longitudinal Study of Procrastination, Performance, Stress, and Health: The Costs & Benefits of Dawdling. *Psychological Science.*

[137] Sirois, F.M., & Tosti, N. (2012). Lost in the moment? An Investigation of Procrastination, Mindfulness, & Well-being. *Journal of Rational-Emotional and Cognitive-Behavior Therapy.*

[138] Buser, T., & Peter, N. (2012). Multitasking. *Experimental Economics.*

[139] Ophir, E., Nass, C., & Wagner, A.D. (2009). Cognitive control in media multitaskers. PNAS.

[140] Kubu, C., & Machado, A. (2017). *The Science is Clear: Why Multitasking Doesn't Work.*

[141] Baker, Z.G., LeRoy, A., & Krieger, H. (2016). Fear of missing out: Relationships with depression, mindfulness, and physical symptoms. *Translational Issues in Psychological Science.*

[142] Rampton, J. (2017). *7 Reasons Why Spending Money on Experiences Makes Us Happier Than Buying Stuff.*

[143] Waters, B. (2011). *The Paradox of Mindfulness and Future Planning.*

[144] Maidenberg, M. (2015). *6 Tips for Making BEST Mindful Decisions.*